TOUCH
RUGBY

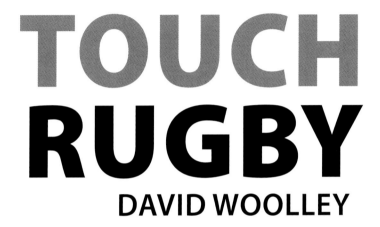

TOUCH
RUGBY

DAVID WOOLLEY

BLOOMSBURY

LONDON • NEW DELHI • NEW YORK • SYDNEY

Published by Bloomsbury Publishing Plc
50 Bedford Square
London WC1B 3DP
www.bloomsbury.com

Bloomsbury is a trademark of Bloomsbury Publishing Plc

First edition 2014

ISBN (print): 978-1-4729-0242-9
ISBN (ePdf): 978-1-4729-0243-6
ISBN (EPUB): 978-1-4729-0244-3

A CIP catalogue record for this book is available from the British Library.

Acknowledgements
Cover and inside photographs © Grant Pritchard, with the exception of the initial photos for Chapters 1 and 2, the final photo in Chapter 2, and the third photo in Chapter 5 © Lynne Cameron/PA Wire; the initial photo for Chapter 3 and the final photo in Chapter 9 © Ross Land/Getty Images; the initial photo for Chapter 6 © Gareth Copley/PA Wire; and the initial photo for Chapter 9 © Nicholas Rjabow/Shutterstock.
Illustrations from original cut-outs by David Gardner
Commissioned by Kirsty Schaper

This book is produced using paper that is made from wood grown in managed, sustainable forests. It is natural, renewable and recyclable. The logging and manufacturing processes conform to the environmental regulations of the ountry of origin.

Typeset in 10pt on 15pt Myriad Pro by Margaret Brain, Wisbech, Cambs
Printed and bound in China by Toppan Leefung Printing
10 9 8 7 6 5 4 3 2 1

CONTENTS

PREFACE

Touch rugby is a game anyone can play. With contact removed – and therefore the possibility of running through the opposition by virtue of force – the focus of the game is passing, catching and lines of running, moving defenders out of position so that the attacking side can score. In the UK any form of rugby where a touch takes the place of a tackle has often been called 'touch' by those who have played it, leading to wide variations in the playing rules adopted at schools and rugby clubs across the country. It takes some people by surprise to learn that touch is not simply a rugby derivative with many forms but a codified, global sport governed by the Federation of International Touch (FIT) and with a large – and growing – player base. The 2010 Australian Sport Commission's survey 'Participation in Exercise, Recreation and Sport' placed touch in the top ten organised physical activities in the country, with a 15 per cent increase in participation since 2001. It is touch as codified by FIT that is played at the quadrennial Touch World Cups; the biannual European and Home Nations Championships; and in domestic leagues across the world.

Touch rugby has specific rules regarding the number of players (six on the field at any one time); the number of touches available to a side (following the sixth touch in a set of possession the ball is given to the defensive team for their attacking 'set' of six touches); the play-the-ball following a touch (ball to be placed on the floor within one stride of where the touch was effected with the hips passing over the ball parallel to the score-lines); and defence (following a touch the defensive team must retreat five metres before they can legally influence play). There is no kicking in touch. Official touch competitions have women's, men's and mixed grades (where at least three players on the field of play must be female) at Open and Senior categories.

FIT works with national organisations such as the England Touch Association (ETA) to run training and qualification courses for players, coaches and referees to enable the global growth of a rationalised sport to provide development pathways in the women's, men's and mixed divisions. These range from social participation all the way up to international level. I have been involved with international touch since 2006, playing in four European

Championships and two World Cups; as a coach I led the England Men's Open side at two European Championships and the 2011 World Cup. As the ETA's Head of Elite Coaching I coordinated England's international and national level coaches in winning the 2012 European team championship and the 2013 Home Nations team championship.

The aims of this book are threefold. First, to encourage informed involvement in touch at a participation level; it is a fun sport that develops health and fitness in an enjoyable environment where gender and age are not of primary importance. Second, to provide coaches and players of contact-based rugby with an understanding of touch. This may lead to their further involvement in the sport, but at the very least the skills and drills outlined here can be incorporated into contact-based rugby training. Touch's emphasis on core skills performed at speed; the requirement to exploit space with the ball in hand; and the necessity for players to run the correct channel in attack makes it the perfect training ground for refining effective attack skills. Without contact, players have to work harder to create openings in a defence through which to score; simply put, playing touch makes people better at contact-based rugby. Benji Marshall and Shaun Johnson represented New Zealand in touch before playing international rugby league and Drumayne Dayberg-Muir captained Australia at the 2007 Touch World Cup before going on to represent Australia on the IRB sevens circuit. At an international level, Australia and New Zealand are the top two touch nations. It is surely no coincidence that they also have an outstanding record in producing individuals and teams with world-leading ball-handling ability within contact rugby; after all, their player pool has a background in competition-honed attack skills where size is not the primary consideration.

Third, this book provides guidance, advice and insight to players and coaches for whom touch is their primary sport. For those who are less experienced, the early sections deal with foundational skills and principles around which the sport is based. The later chapters aim to provide some approaches to tactical game management and patterns of play that can be used as they are articulated here but that will ideally form a sounding board for coaches and players to formulate and refine their own ideas and approaches as they consider, debate and critique them. This is the book I wish had been available when I first started playing touch.

1

GETTING STARTED – SIMPLIFIED PLAYING RULES

The following is a basic summary of the rules of touch. While more technical aspects of certain rules are discussed in later chapters, this outline should enable players and coaches totally new to the sport to play the game in essentially the same fashion as the final of an international tournament.

Scoring

A try or touchdown is scored by a member of the attacking team (as long as they are not the 'acting half') placing the ball in a controlled manner over the score-line they are attacking. As there are no other ways of scoring points in touch other than a try or touchdown each score counts as 'one.' The team with the most scores wins the game.

Passing

A player may pass, throw, tap or deliver the ball in any other way to any member of the attacking side as long as the ball does not go forward or touch the ground.

Possession of the ball

Teams take it in turns to have possession. A set of possession is called a 'set of six' as the members of the team in possession can only be touched a maximum of six times by the players in the defence. A change of possession will occur when;

- a try is scored (tap restart on the halfway line);

- the sixth touch occurs;

- the ball touches the ground;

- the acting half is touched in possession of the ball;

- the acting half places the ball over the score-line;

- the ball-carrier steps on or over the perimeter of the playing area;

- a roll ball or tap restart are performed incorrectly.

Making the touch

A touch is affected through ANY contact between the ball-carrier and a member of the defending team (the team not in possession of the ball). Minimum force should be used to make the touch and the referee will punish excessive force. The touch can be affected by the ball-carrier touching a defender. It is the practice for the defender who made the touch to call 'touch' to ensure that the referee is aware that a touch has been made. It is standard practice for the referee to accept the defender's word that they have made a touch unless the referee observes that contact was not made. In this circumstance, a penalty will be given to the attacking side and the defender may be sin-binned for calling a 'phantom touch'.

The roll ball

When a touch has been affected the ball-carrier restarts play through executing a roll ball. The ball is placed on the ground between the legs with the hips parallel to the score-line being attacked. The hips must pass over the ball before it can be picked up by another member of the attacking team. The ball cannot roll back more than one metre when it is placed on the ground and the roll ball cannot be delayed. The ball-carrier must play the ball within the stride they were taking as they were touched or they will be penalised for 'going over the mark'.

The tap restart

The game is started (and restarted after each try is scored and at the start of the second half) with a tap on the halfway line. Any attacking player places the ball on the ground, takes both hands off the ball and taps it with their foot. The ball may not travel a distance greater than one metre before it is picked up cleanly by the attacker who tapped it. At the tap, the defence must be at least ten metres away from the mark where the ball is being tapped. Apart from this there is no kicking of any kind in touch – no kick offs, no kicks to the side-line and no conversions of a try or touchdown.

Penalties

When a penalty is given by the referee it is taken in exactly the same manner outlined for the tap with the ball placed on the ground where the referee has given the penalty mark.

The team being penalised must retreat ten metres from the mark established by the referee. Penalties are awarded for;

- a forward pass;

- a touch and pass where the player is touched and then passes the ball rather than executing a roll ball (this is at the discretion of the referee who may judge that the ball was in the process of being passed as the touch was made);

- a roll ball being performed over the mark;

- the defence being offside at the roll ball (nearer than five metres from the mark);

- the defence being offside at the tap (nearer than ten metres from the mark);

- a team having more than six players on the field;

- falsely claiming a touch has been made;

- using excessive force to make the touch;

- incorrect substitution;

- other misconduct.

Offside/onside

When a touch has been effected, the entire defence must retreat five metres towards the score-line they are defending from the 'mark' where the roll ball is being played, or to the score-line itself (if it is less than five metres from the mark). In the latter circumstance the ball-carrier can retreat to a point that is five metres away from the score-line before playing the ball if they wish.

The acting half

Following the roll ball, whichever member of the attacking side picks up the ball is known as the acting half until they have passed to another player. For as long as the player who picks up the ball is the acting half (that is, until they have passed the ball) they cannot score and if they are touched while still in possession of the ball then the defending team will be granted possession. If the half passes the ball immediately following the roll ball and then receives it back they are not considered to be the acting half; they may score and if they are touched by a defender it is considered to be a normal touch.

Playing numbers

Each side can field a maximum of six players at any one time. In a game of mixed touch, the rules state that a minimum of three players on the field at all times must be female and at least one must be male; in practice all sides play three men and three women. The two players in the middle of the six on the field are known as the 'middles'; the two players on the extreme left and right are known as 'wings'; and the players in between each middle and each wing are known as the 'links'.

Substitutions

There are no limits on the number of times a player can leave and re-enter the field of play. Substitutions must occur within the team's substitution box, an area 20 metres in length situated on both sides of the field at halfway. In many sides each player has a sub-buddy with one player staying on the field for an average of two attacking sets of six and two defensive sets before leaving the field to be replaced by their 'buddy' who does the same. This constant work-rest interval (one set of six takes approximately 45 seconds to complete) enables the pace of the game to remain extremely high.

The playing field

A touch field is 70 metres long from score-line to score-line and 50 metres wide. From the score-line to the dead ball line there is a five-metre-deep score zone.

Duration

A game consists of two halves of 20 minutes duration.

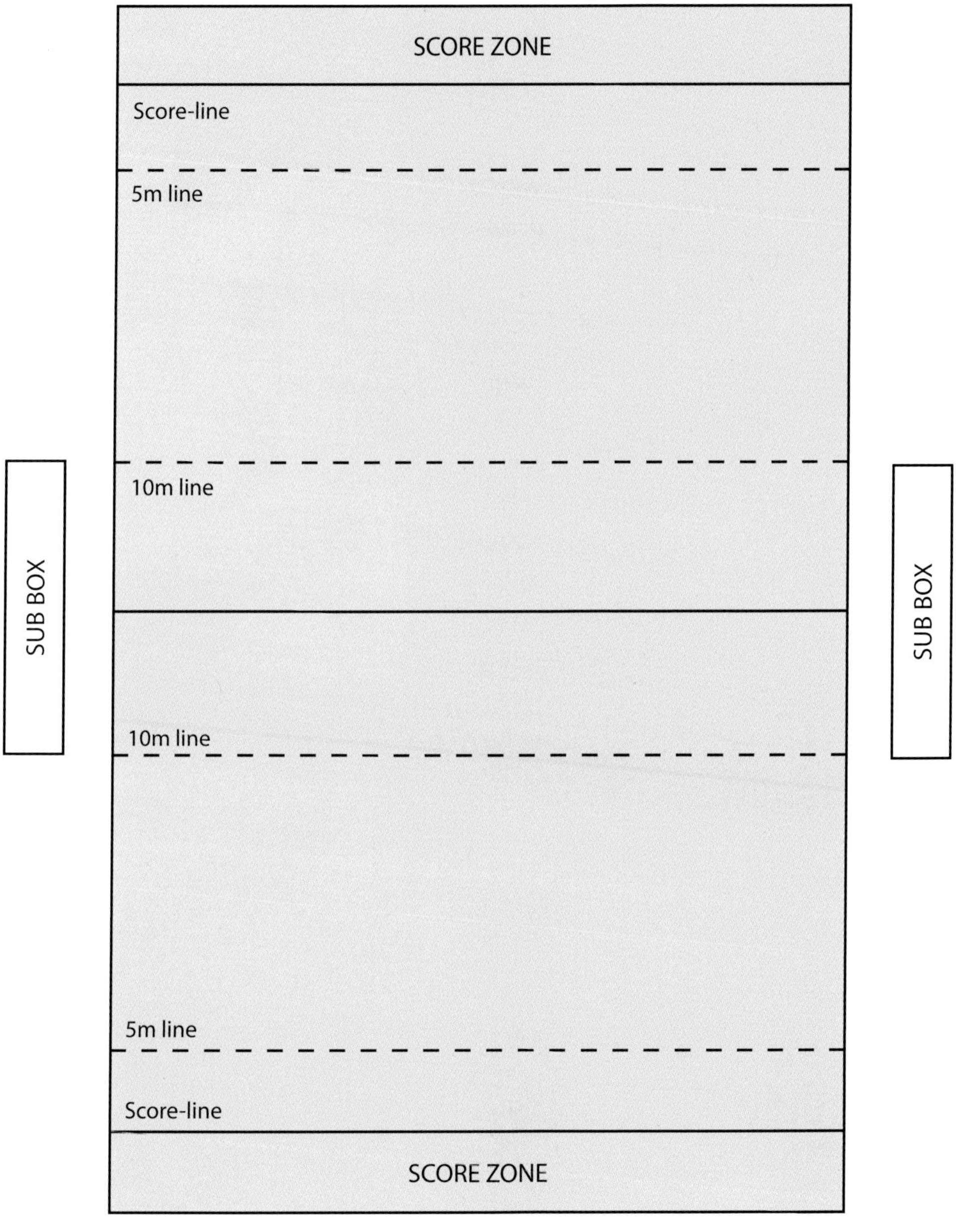

SCORE ZONE

Score-line

5m line

10m line

SUB BOX

SUB BOX

10m line

5m line

Score-line

SCORE ZONE

Figure 1.1 The dimensions of a touch field and its markings

2 ACQUIRING POSSESSION SKILLS

This chapter explains the core skills required when in possession of the ball. The names of skills and the design of the drills are specific to touch, but in many cases are similar to other forms of rugby. Players and coaches should have in mind that touch is an invasion game (like rugby union) but with possession guaranteed to the opposition on the completion of the sixth touch or an incomplete phase of play (like rugby league). Basic attack skills are important because 'completion' of sets of possession (retaining the ball until a try is scored or the sixth touch is effected) is the only way a side can achieve a greater level of possession than their opponents. The fewer mistakes a side makes when in possession of the ball, the more opportunities they will have to score; the more mistakes a side makes, the more time they will spend defending, and the more liable they will be to conceding.

Basic passing

Touch depends on effective movement of the ball back and forth across the attacking line. Possession of the ball is surrendered – known as a turnover of possession – as soon as it touches the ground. Therefore the ability to pass off both hands is a core touch skill for every player.

END-OVER-END PASSING

The easiest pass to make and to receive is an end-over-end pass. Hold the ball in two hands at opposite sides of the fatter part of the ball, palms underneath the ball and facing up, thumbs on top of the ball and facing down. The two middle fingers should be approximately halfway up the length of the ball. Point the tip of the ball towards the target and face the target chest-on. Flick the wrists to generate the momentum of the pass, pushing down with the thumbs so that the ball travels towards the target with backspin, end-over-end. For an easier pass to catch, flick the ball less dynamically so that it rotates more slowly and travels higher in the air.

Figure 2.1 Illustration of an end-over-end pass.

DRILL 1

Create a ten-metre by ten-metre square. Place one player on each corner with a ball and a player without the ball in the middle of the square (resembling a number five on a die). Each of the players on a corner takes it in turn to pass the ball to the player in the middle, executing the end-over-end pass. The player in the middle catches the ball before passing it back to the player from whom they have received it, practising the skill. After the desired period of time, rotate the positions of the players.

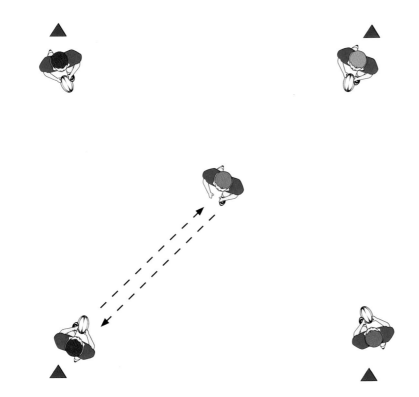

Figure 2.2 Drill to develop end-over-end passing.

To develop the drill, have the players on the edge of the square pass the ball in a non-sequential order; alternatively, have only one ball in the square, with the player in the middle deciding who to pass it to once they have received it.

DRILL 2

Create a ten-metre by ten-metre square and place at least two players on each cone. Place a ball with the first player on the top left cone and the first player on the bottom right cone. The ball-carriers advance to the middle of the square at which point they pass to the player on the cone at 90 degrees to their left, practising the skill. The player who has just passed the ball continues their run to the cone diagonally opposite to them. The player who has received the ball repeats the drill.

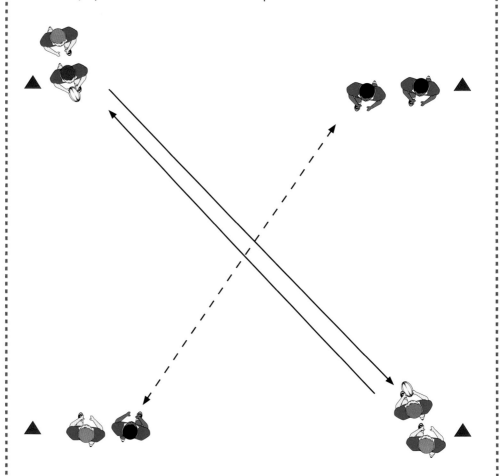

Figure 2.3 Drill to develop end-over-end passing while on the move.

To develop passing off the right hand, players should pass the ball to their right. To increase the difficulty of the drill, a ball can be given to the first player at each corner of the square; they all simultaneously move to the middle of the square and execute their pass. To develop the drill further a player is given possession of the ball and stands at cone A (as shown in Figure 2.4). They advance along the side of the square to cone B (on their right); just before halfway between the two cones they pass the ball to a player who has begun to advance along the side of the square from cones B to C. The receiver catches the pass and immediately delivers a pass to a player advancing along the side of the square from cones C to D, etc. Once a player has passed the ball they remain at the cone they have run to, waiting to repeat the skill.

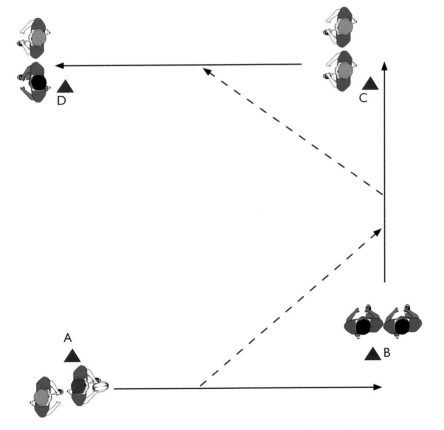

Figure 2.4 Passing and moving along the sides of a square towards a moving target.

SPIN PASSING

Spin passes enable players to deliver a longer pass with greater accuracy and more speed than an end-over-end pass. Spin passes may be executed in open play and are also regularly used by the acting half (the player who picks the ball up from the ground when a ruck has been executed). It is worth remembering that wet and windy playing conditions can make the spin pass difficult to execute and to catch.

Passing to the left

When passing from the ground (as an acting half) the player positions their right foot to the right-hand side of the ball, flexing their right knee and adopting a secure position over the ball. Side-on to the player they are passing to, the passer picks up the ball in two hands, each on opposite sides of the fatter part of the ball. The player places their right hand at the bottom half of the ball (furthest from the player to whom they are passing) and the left hand at the top half of the ball (nearest the player to whom they are passing). They point the narrow tip of the ball towards the target. As they take a stride towards the target with their left foot they transfer their weight from the flexed right leg to their left. They push down on the ball with the left thumb, simultaneously pushing up with the right palm and fingers so

Figure 2.5 Illustration of a spin pass to the left.

that the hands cross. They should follow through so that the right hand ends up by the left shoulder and the left hand by the right hip as they finish transferring their weight from the right to the left leg.

The further a player wishes to pass the ball, the more dynamic the action and follow-through need to be. On the follow-through the hands should finish further away from the body, sending the ball a greater distance. Sometimes a larger 'wind up' – drawing back the hands and arms to generate power – before delivering the pass may be required. However, the more power generated from the dynamism of the action and follow-through the better, as a larger 'wind up' telegraphs that a longer pass is going to be attempted.

Passing to the right

When passing from the ground as an acting half the same technique is adopted as outlined above but with the left and right elements reversed. Thus the player positions their left foot to the left-hand side of the ball, flexing their left knee and adopting a secure position over the ball. Side-on to the player they are passing to the passer picks up the ball in two hands, each on opposite sides of the fatter part of the ball. The player places their left hand at the

Figure 2.6 Illustration of a spin pass to the right.

bottom half of the ball (furthest from the player to whom they are passing) and the right hand at the top half of the ball (nearest the player to whom they are passing). They point the narrow tip of the ball towards the target. As they take a stride towards the target with their right foot they transfer their weight from the flexed left leg to their right. They push down on the ball with the right thumb, simultaneously pushing up with the left palm and fingers so that the hands cross. They should follow through so that the left hand ends up by the right shoulder and the right hand by the left hip as they finish transferring their weight from the left to the right leg.

DRILL 3

Place four cones in a straight line with the second cone five metres from the first; the third cone five metres from the second; and the fourth five metres from the third. At the second, third and fourth cones place a ball to the left of the cone. At 90 degrees to the left of the first cone in the line, place a second cone five metres from the first; the third five metres from the second; and the fourth five metres from the third, again in a direct line. Have at least one player lined up behind each of the four cones that do not have a ball next to them facing forwards (up the right-angled grid towards the balls). The player at the cone directly behind the line of balls approaches the first ball and the player behind the second cone moves forward to receive a spin pass from the ground, running through the grid once they have caught the pass; the passer moves forwards to the next cone and executes a longer spin pass to the player standing behind the third cone who again moves forward to receive the pass and runs through the grid having caught the ball. The passer then moves forward to the next cone and delivers a long spin pass to the player standing behind the fourth cone, who moves forward to receive it and runs through the grid having caught the ball. The players bring the balls back to the cones and change positions in the grid.

Encourage the passer to deliver a flat pass from each cone (rather than passing at the cone the receiver is standing on) so that they become used to passing the ball into space (and anticipating where the runner will receive it); encourage the runners to run on to the ball so that they are used to receiving a ball at pace. This will encourage players in a game situation to take the pass as close to the gain line as possible meaning that they receive a pass that has gone backwards but is as close to the lateral

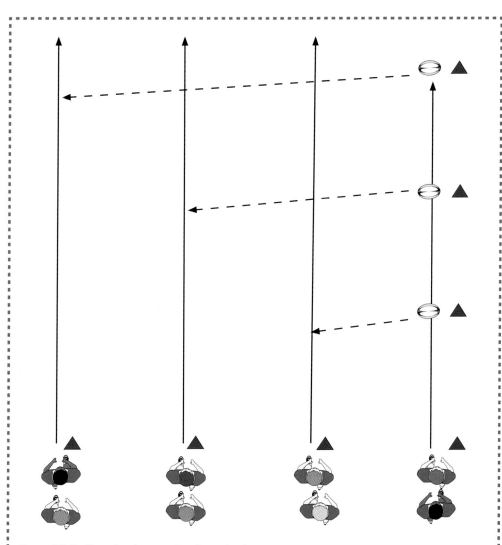

Figure 2.7 Drill to develop passing from the floor.

line of the roll ball as possible. To develop passing off the right hand, simply move the balls so that they are inside the second, third and fourth cones that the players have just been running from and get the players to line up on the empty cones to the right of the line of balls. To develop the drill, change the order in which the passes are delivered (for example, the middle pass followed by the longest pass, followed by the shortest pass).

Rucking – the roll ball

The ruck (or roll ball) is a vital touch skill. A team that can catch, pass and roll the ball effectively will be able to offer a challenge to most sides they encounter. However, as with basic passing and catching, the roll ball is often overlooked in training as coaches look to develop more complicated (but less important or effective) ways of playing. The primary aim of rucking is to advance the ball up the field as quickly as possible while using the fewest number of touches. If executed correctly it is the simplest way to catch a defence offside – which in turn creates opportunities to score.

To execute a roll ball with the greatest efficiency, a one-handed grip can be an advantage (freeing the spare hand to initiate the touch on the defender). Official touch rugby balls used in international competitions are roughly equivalent to a rugby union size 4 ball. They are manufactured by Steeden (suppliers to rugby league's Super League) and have a similarly fatter, rounder shape than those used in union. Players with larger hands will be able to hold the ball horizontally in one hand with an overhand grip; players with smaller hands may find it necessary to cradle the ball in one hand. However, control of the ball is the highest consideration so if necessary the player rucking the ball should use two hands to place it on the floor.

Figure 2.8 Cradlling the ball in one hand while initiating the touch.

Figure 2.9 Holding the ball with an overhand grip while initiating the touch.

A ruck can only be executed when the ball-carrier is touched by a member of the defending team; the ball-carrier can themselves initiate the touch so as to place the ball on the ground at a place and time they can influence. The ball must be placed on the ground as soon as a player is touched. This must be executed within the stride the ball-carrier was taking as contact was made between them and the defender. When the ball is placed on the ground the ball-carrier must advance so that it passes between their legs with their hips square to the score-line they are attacking. The ball should be placed securely on the floor to make it easier for the attacking player picking up the ball (the acting half).

Figure 2.10 Initiating the touch and rucking the ball – face on.

Figure 2.11 Initiating the touch and rucking the ball – from the side.

Attacking teams often lose possession at the ruck in a variety of ways. A common error is 'going over the mark' – placing the ball on the ground within a stride after the one they were taking as they were touched. Another issue can be 'loss of control' or 'ball to ground', general phrases that cover dropping the ball while attempting to place it on the ground; placing the ball carelessly, causing it to move on the ground in a manner that leads the referee to judge control has been lost; or players kicking the ball as they advance over it after placing it on the ground. These errors are often avoidable through a good grip (as outlined on pages 32 and 33) and effective practice of solid rucking technique.

Where possible, the attacking team should initiate the touch in order to help them avoid 'going over the mark'; if players have a better idea of when they will be touched they can anticipate with greater certainty where they will have to ruck the ball. When approaching the defender on whom they will initiate the touch, the ball-carrier should determine which of their hands will be closer to the defender and initiate the touch with that hand. The ball-carrier should not initiate the touch with the hand that is carrying the ball; if necessary they should transfer the ball to the hand furthest from the defender in the strides before the touch. This will help the ball-carrier avoid jarring on the ball-carrying hand or arm, which can lead to loss of control issues. If a player can only keep the ball secure by holding it in two hands they can still initiate the touch by making contact with the defender by touching them with the ball before placing it on the ground.

Whether it is achieved with the spare hand or with the ball itself, the ball-carrier should look to ruck to the side of the defender; this will help attackers gain a performance advantage as the defender must retreat five metres from where the ball is placed after the touch has been made. If the ball is to the side of the defender (or even behind), the distance of retreat may be five or six metres, giving the attackers a greater opportunity of catching the defence offside. The ball-carrier should plant one foot on the same side as the ball-carrying hand as they make contact with the defender so that they can adopt a low 'driving' position. This will enable them to keep the ball safe; ensure a wide, strong stance with the legs that contact with the defender will not disrupt (increasing the likelihood of loss of control issues); and make it obvious to the referee that when the ball is firmly placed on the floor next to the foot that takes the next stride that they have not gone 'over the mark'.

DRILL 4

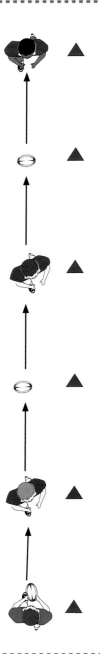

Place six cones in a line, ten metres apart; one defender stands at the second cone, one at the fourth and one at the sixth. A ball is placed at the third and fifth cones. A player stands at the first cone with a ball in hand and runs towards the defender at the second cone, where they initiate the touch and execute the roll ball. The player continues to run towards the third cone, picking up the ball as they pass, before repeating the skill on the next defender on the fourth cone. The player repeats the routine, scooping up the ball at the fifth cone and initiating the roll ball on the defender at the sixth. The focus of the drill is the roll ball; defenders should be passive and not move off the cone they are on to allow attackers to hone the skill. However, as a development of the drill, defenders can be instructed to move forward from their position as soon as the attacker has scooped up the ball – this replicates what would happen in a game situation and places pressure on the attacker to make decisions about which hand they will use to initiate the touch and which hand they will use to roll the ball.

Figure 2.12 Drill to practise the roll ball.

DRILL 5

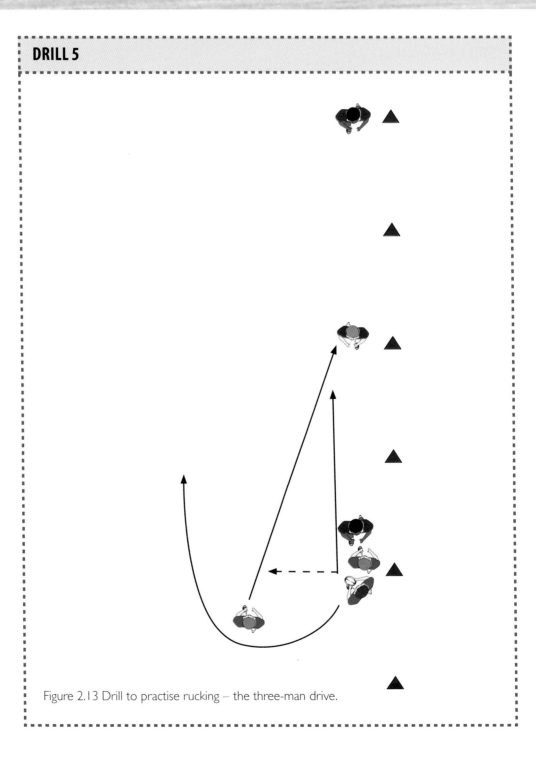

Figure 2.13 Drill to practise rucking – the three-man drive.

As in Drill 4, place six cones in a line, ten metres apart; one defender stands at the second cone, one at the fourth and one at the sixth. Three players stand at the first cone, one with the ball in hand. The ball-carrier runs towards the defender at the second cone where they initiate the touch and execute the roll ball. Once the first touch has been made, the first phase of play has ended and the second phase has begun. Teams at higher levels of touch will increasingly be concerned with multi-phase playing and this is discussed in later chapters. The player nearest the ruck is the acting half and passes off the ground to the third attacker, who runs on to the ball. The new ball-carrier ends this phase of play by initiating the touch on the next defender at the fourth cone; the initial ball-carrier moves forward to become the acting half and the initial acting half is the next runner (having followed their pass and run around the initial runner – this angle of running is called a wrap). When the runner receives the ball they approach the defender on the last cone and execute the ruck; the player who executed the ruck on the previous defender becomes the acting half and the player who was the acting half at the second ruck becomes the next runner. When the runner receives the ball from the ruck on the final defender they run through the grid and the drill is over. This method of rucking the ball with three players rotating positions is known as the 'three-man drive'.

Angles of running in attack

Dragging – sometimes called 'dragging out' – describes a line of running commonly adopted by the ball-carrier in the attacking half of the field. The ball-carrier attacks the channel of space on the side of the defender who is marking them where there are fewest other defenders. This is known as attacking the 'outside'.

Figure 2.14 The ball-carrier identifies which shoulder of the defender has the fewest other defenders between it and the side-line. This is the 'outside' of the defender marking the ball-carrier, and the ball-carrier moves forward into this space.

DRILL 6

It is important to stress to players that they are attacking space – not simply running straight at the defender. To encourage players to attack the space, create a 20-metre (length) by 15-metre (width) rectangle. Place two cones on one side of the rectangle – cone B at six metres and cone C at nine metres (as shown in Figure 2.15 opposite). One attacker with the ball stands at cone B and one defender stands at cone C. On the coach's command, the attacker runs from cone B to cone A, turns 90 degrees around the cone and attempts to score by placing the ball over the line at the far end of the rectangle. Simultaneously, the defender runs from cone C to cone D, turns around the cone and attempts to make the touch on the attacker before they score. The drill should naturally encourage the attacker to run to the outside of the defender as this makes the most of their advantage from the head start. This drill can be developed by changing the size of the rectangle and the distances the attackers and defenders run before turning the corner.

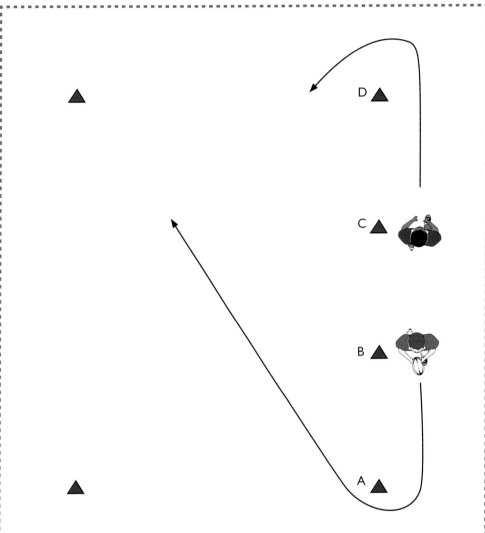

Figure 2.15 One-versus-one drill to develop attacking the defender on their outside.

DRILL 7

Create two 20-metre (length) by 15-metre (width) rectangles side by side, with a five-metre gap between them, as shown in Figure 2.16. A team of two defenders stand in the middle of each channel, attempting to prevent two attackers from scoring; neither defender can leave their rectangle. The ball-carrier – who imagines they are a link with a winger outside them – is encouraged to sharply accelerate and attack the five-metre 'safe' channel. If the ball-carrier attacks the space effectively then they should beat the defender and accelerate through the safe channel to score. If the defender opposite the other attacker stops defending against their player and tries to stop the ball-carrier scoring by stepping in towards the safe channel, the ball-carrier should pass to their fellow attacker (standing wide in space) who will score.

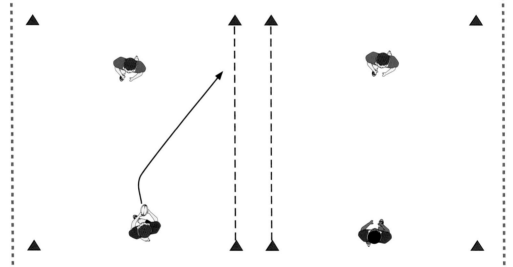

Figure 2.16 Imagining they are the link with four attackers on their left-hand side helps the ball-carrier and all the other players to appreciate that the 'outside' channel is being attacked.

The ball-carrier can execute the angle of running outlined on page 40 and be unable to get into space on the side of the defender where there are fewest other defenders. In the early stages of a game, when all the players are fresh, this is a likely outcome of the drag. If the defender is not beaten by the drag, an option for the ball-carrier is to initiate the touch on the defender and ruck the ball (drag-down). The more effectively the ball-carrier has attacked the space outside their defender, the more the defender will have had to chase out across the field to cover them, taking their fellow defenders with them. This will have created space on the opposite side of the pitch. The attacking team will therefore wish to play the ball as quickly as possible and transfer the point of attack to where the space has emerged.

DRAG-DOWN

When the ball-carrier (ideally the middle) and their nearest teammate on their outside (ideally their link) realise that the chasing defender is not going to be beaten, they communicate with each other that the ball-carrier is going to 'go down'. This means they will initiate the touch on the chasing defender and ruck the ball before 'splitting' laterally with their momentum and slightly backwards from the place where the ball was rucked, offering themselves as an option for the acting half to pass to. In this circumstance the acting half uses the splitting player as a dummy option and passes away from the splitter to the middle on the other side of the field who will attack the space created by the defence moving to cover the first phase of play. In the words of my first touch coach, 'attack right to score left; attack left to score right'.

DRILL 8

Create a 15-metre by 15-metre square as shown in Figure 2.17; a minimum of five players should stand at cones A and D and a minimum of two players should stand at cones B and C. A ball should be placed at cone A and the first player scoops up the ball and runs up and across to cone C. The first player at cone D marks the ball-carrier; the ball-carrier looks to initiate the touch on the defender having dragged them across the square before executing an accurate roll ball. The ball-carrier then splits towards the defence's outside (the same direction they have dragged towards); the first player on cone B moves forward to become the acting half, dummies a pass to the splitting ball-carrier and then passes to the next player on cone A who moves forward to receive the ball. Having caught the ball, they place it at cone D. The passer and receiver join cone D and the splitter and defender join cone C. The drill is then repeated coming back down the rectangle. To practise the skill passing off the other hand, place the ball at cone B and ensure that there is a minimum of five players at cones B and C and a minimum of two players at cones A and D.

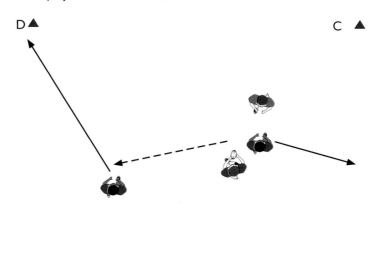

Figure 2.17 Drill to practise drag-down.

MAXIMISING OVERLAPS

Dragging (a player moving into the space on the shoulder of a defender where they have fewest fellow defenders) is a core pattern of play in touch because it is the simplest method by which an overlap may be created, for example, the middle attacks the outside shoulder of their defender and beats them for pace, creating a three-on-two attacking overlap. In overlap scenarios, the ball-carrier must straighten into the gap they find themselves in, that is, with forward momentum they angle towards the defender who has just been beaten.

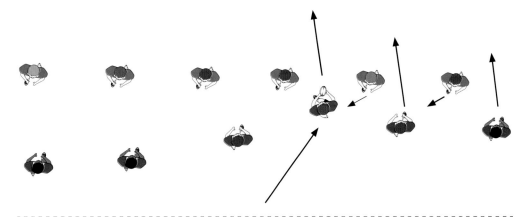

Figure 2.18 The ball-carrying middle has beaten the defender marking them on the side where the defender has fewest fellow defenders. This has created a three-on-two attacking overlap.

Although straightening may feel counter-intuitive, the effect is to pull the remaining defenders away from the other attackers; once an overlap has been created then the attackers on the side of the field of the overlap should be attacking the channel outside their defender. If the ball-carrier straightens and pulls the defence infield, the outside attacker will not have to work as hard to be in the right position to exploit the numbers advantage.

DRILL 9

Create a ten-metre by ten-metre square with one attacker at both cones A and B and one defender at cone C (as shown below). The ball is held by the attacker at cone A. The ball-carrier moves towards the middle of the square and then straightens, accelerating towards cone D. This mimics the running angle of beating a defender on their outside before straightening into the channel. The defender moves forward from cone C and attempts to make the touch on the ball-carrier. If they fail, the ball-carrier moves forward and scores. If the defender looks likely to catch the ball-carrier, the ball is passed to the attacker moving forward from cone B, who moves forward and scores.

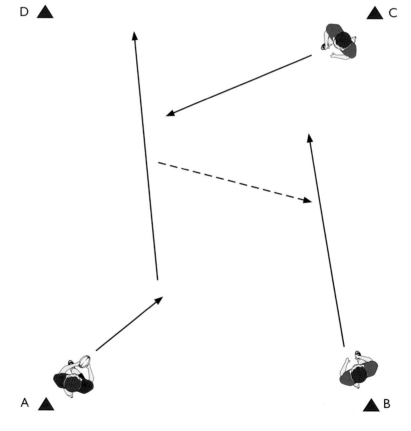

Figure 2.19 Drill to develop two-versus-one overlap execution.

DRILL 10

Create a 20-metre by 20-metre square with cone B placed seven metres and cone C placed ten metres up the right-hand side, as shown below. Attackers stand behind cone B, defenders stand behind cone C. On the coach's signal, two attackers (one already holding the ball) run down to cone A and one defender runs up to cone D. Having turned 90 degrees around cone A, the attackers move forward and attempt to score over the line at the far end of the square. The defender, having turned around cone D, tries to prevent them from doing so.

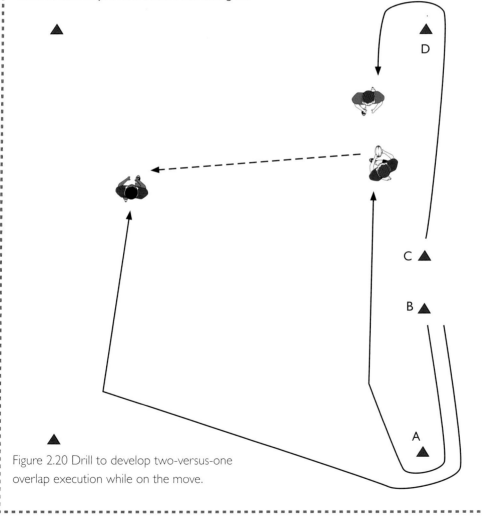

Figure 2.20 Drill to develop two-versus-one overlap execution while on the move.

The purpose of the drill is to create an overlap scenario where all the players are moving; the attackers are therefore challenged to identify the correct channel in which to run in a live situation. The ball-carrier should angle in and attack the corner as the defender turns around to enter the square. This is the equivalent of the ball-carrier in a game straightening and pulling the defence infield. The other attacker should stay wide and receive the ball on the gain line – as they should in a match. The attackers maximise their chances of scoring by running the lines they should run in a game; the defender should not be able to stop the attackers scoring, but will gain experience of scrambling in defence. To increase the level of challenge for the attackers – and to give the drill a more defensive focus – a second defender can be sent into the square after a short delay; this is the equivalent of defenders chasing across to cover the overlap in a game scenario. The attackers should not do anything different – but it does place them under greater pressure in executing the skill.

3 ACQUIRING DEFENSIVE SKILLS

The rules of touch favour the attacking side. Teams should have the ambition of not conceding; yet a perfect defensive system does not exist and if an attacking side is effective and accurate then they are likely to score at some point in a match. Therefore the mindset of teams should be to make the act of scoring as difficult as possible; if a score is conceded, the defence should ensure that the attacking side has had to do something positively good to score (rather than gifting them an opportunity through errors or lack of effort). Defence is a collective endeavour; individual defenders must work hard to stand close to each other, protecting the channels between them. By collectively forming a narrow barrier, a defence will protect the area of the field it covers as a group, denying attackers the opportunity to accelerate into spaces having received a short and simple pass.

The aim of both the defence and the attack is to control the roll ball (also known as the ruck) so as to influence the speed of the play. The attack want to recycle the ball as quickly as possible in order to reduce the time the defence has to organise; the defence wish the roll ball to be as slow as possible in order to set themselves in position. Some approaches that can help players to defend more effectively within the rules include:

- anticipating the touch so that when a fellow defender makes it they are already getting themselves back onside;

- making the touch with the hand that is on the side where there are more defenders – this will help the defender retreat at an angle protecting the short side (where there are fewer defenders);

- retreating while facing forwards (where possible) so that the actions of the attack can be observed and do not take the defence by surprise.

Defending the ruck in midfield

Any contact between the attacker and defender – no matter who initiates it – is a touch. While attackers may look to initiate the touch, the defender should aim to touch the attacker in order to influence the timing and position of the roll ball and to seize the initiative in the ruck (rather than allow the attacker to initiate the touch on the defender). When the defender touches the attacker they should assertively call 'touch' to inform the referee that a touch has been made and again generate a sense that they have the initiative in the contact situation.

In addition to the above there are a number of other ways in which a defender can make the touch to gain a competitive advantage over the attacker. These include:

- making the touch when positioned between the attacker and the score-line, for example, in front of the player with the ball;

- making the touch on the attacker before the attacker gets into the low drive position to ruck the ball – this gives the defender extra time to retreat before the acting half plays the ball;

- using the attacker's momentum to aid their retreat five metres back from the ruck – thus saving energy – which is particularly achievable in midfield as the attack looks to gain field position and runners accelerate into the ruck.

The defence aims to 'turn the ball over' and gain possession of the ball while conceding as little territory as possible. This can be achieved by pressurising the attack into an error through retreating five metres as quickly as possible and then advancing to reduce the space. However, the defence also wants to avoid the opposition having repeat sets of six; so

Figure 3.1 Making the touch in midfield. The defender making the touch is ready to move to his left, protecting the short side, while his fellow defender is anticipating covering the gap between them.

it is vital that a defence does not give away penalties to the attacking side. Therefore, each defender must be aware that they may only move forward from the position to which they have retreated when the acting half touches the ball. However, if the attacking side delays the roll ball or the roll ball is executed a distance away from a potential acting half, the defending team can ask the referee if they may advance or the referee may tell the defence they may advance without being asked. It is the responsibility of the defence to make sure that the referee judges their advance to be fair, as a penalty will be awarded to the attacking team for offside if not.

If a player affects a touch before they have retreated five metres then the referee will call 'play on'. Even if the defender who made the touch in an offside position then makes it back onside and affects the touch again, this touch will be ignored. This defender is considered out of the game until another player makes a touch from an onside position (at which point the referee will decide whether to continue to play advantage or award a penalty).

DRILL 11

A ball-carrier stands five metres away from a defender. The defender advances and makes the touch on the ball-carrier, aiming to use the tactic outlined above. Having made the touch, the defender retreats five metres; once they reach their starting point, they advance once more to repeat the skill. The defender repeats the skill six times to replicate a set of six; the ball-carrier and the defender then swap roles. This basic drill gives the coach an opportunity to watch an individual's repeated technique to give constructive advice on the retreat from – and advance to – each touch. It also provides a very predictable environment for the defender to develop their technique.

DRILL 12

One defender stands eight metres away from three attackers in the middle of a ten-metre wide channel. Another defender should stand approximately eight metres behind the first and a third defender should stand approximately eight metres behind the second. The three attacking players execute a three-man drive while each of the defenders perfects the ideal method of making the touch. The defenders and the attackers then swap roles.

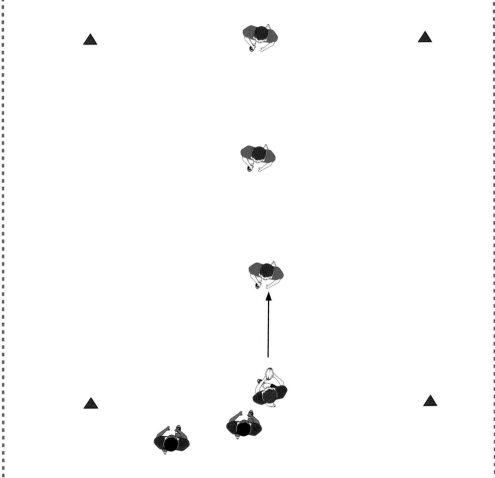

Figure 3.2 A drill developing making the touch in midfield.

A development of this drill is to have only one defender in the channel. The attackers perform the three-man drive and the defender works back five metres from each touch as they would in a game scenario. This creates a more pressurised context for the defender to perfect their technique of making the touch. The defender should be intending to retreat five metres as quickly as possible before advancing and cutting down the space the attacker has, denying the attacking side easily gained yards and putting pressure on the ball-carrier.

Defending against attempts to manoeuvre the defence near to the score-line

The most vulnerable area for a defence is its 'short side'. The short side is determined by which defender has either made the touch or whose channel is being attacked by the ball-carrier at any specific moment; it is the side on which the engaged defender has fewest fellow defenders. It is vulnerable because it is the area of the field on which the attacker can score most straightforwardly by accelerating outside a defender and beating them for pace. Either the ball-carrier will have an opportunity to score themselves or – if there is another defender outside the beaten player – they may draw the other defender and create an overlap. The fewer defenders there are, the fewer the obstacles presented to the attacking team.

Therefore, each defender is responsible for primarily marking a channel (rather than a specific player). A channel is the space between one defender and another, or between a defender and the side-line (if they are positioned on the wing). To protect the short side, the defenders should view the six attacking players as two groups of three; a three on the left and a three on the right (as the defenders look at the attackers). If the ball is in the possession of any attacker in the three on the left, every defender marks the channel between themselves and the player (or side-line if they are a winger) on their left, thus protecting the short side. If the ball is in the possession of any attacker in the three on the right, every defender marks the channel between themselves and the player (or side-line if they are a winger) on their right, thus protecting the short side. In the photo opposite, the left-hand defensive middle has been engaged by the ball-carrier. There are three fellow defenders to his right and two to his left; therefore the short side is to the engaged defender's left.

Figure 3.3 The defence's short side is on the side of the field where the engaged defender has fewest fellow defenders. In this case, the short side is the left-hand side of the defence.

Defenders aim to position themselves between the attacker and the channel the attacker is looking to accelerate into on the short side, dissuading them from doing so by denying them space and forcing them to look towards the defence's 'long side' – the side of the field where the defender engaged by the attacker has the greater number of fellow defenders. Although the attacking winger furthest away from the ball-carrier is standing in space on the outside and the defence is vulnerable to a long pass, throwing longer passes to the other side of the field is inherently more difficult for the attack to execute than attacking the short side. A long pass may have too much flight put on it, giving the defenders time to chase out to the receiver; the pass may be intercepted; or attackers may decide against attempting the pass, judging it to be beyond their capabilities.

The short side can also be protected from the ruck through 'pulling a corner'. This strategy operates on a similar principle; however, on this occasion the six defending players are two groups of three; a three on the left and a three on the right (as the defenders look upfield). If the player who has made the touch is any defender in the three on the left, every defender retreats five metres from the ruck at an angle towards their left-hand corner of the field to close the channel between themselves and the player (or side-line if they are a winger) on their left, thus protecting the short side. If the player who has made the touch is any defender in the three on the right, every defender retreats five metres at an angle from the ruck towards their right-hand corner of the field to close the channel between themselves and the player (or side-line if they are a winger) on their right, thus protecting the short side. In Figure 3.4, the right-hand defensive middle has just made the touch. There are three fellow defenders to their left and two to their right; therefore the short side is to the defender's right and they retreat five metres from the ruck at an angle towards their right-hand defensive corner.

Figure 3.4 With the right-hand defensive middle having made the touch the short side is on the defence's right; therefore they retreat five metres at an angle towards the right-hand defensive corner to protect it from the attacking side.

DRILL 13

Two teams of six face each other in a condensed space (approximately 15 metres deep and 30 metres across). Players on both sides are not allowed to run, only walk. On the attacking side the left-hand middle (as the defence looks upfield at the attack) holds the ball. Every defender marks the channel between themselves and the player (or side-line if they are a winger) on their left. The attackers do not move – but the left-hand middle passes the ball to the right-hand middle (as the defence looks upfield at the attack). Every defender reacts, moving across to mark the channel between themselves and the player (or side-line if they are a winger) on their right, thus protecting the short side. The middles pass the ball to each other when they choose, and the defenders reposition themselves every time that they do.

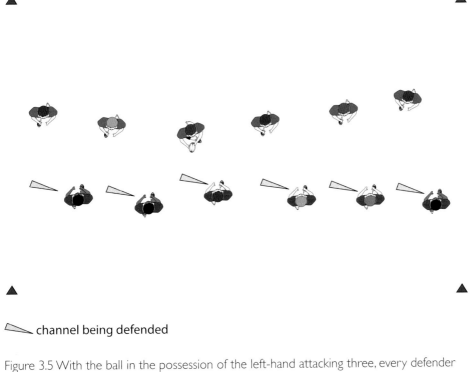

◢ channel being defended

Figure 3.5 With the ball in the possession of the left-hand attacking three, every defender marks the channel between themselves and the player on their left (or the side-line if they are a winger).

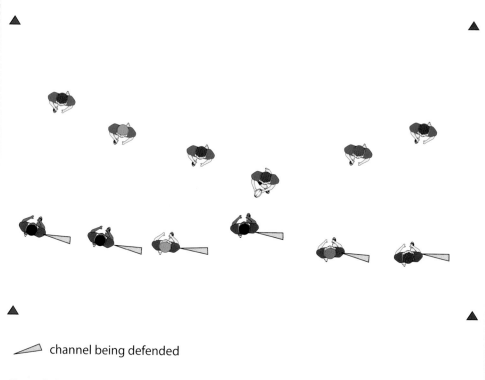

◁ channel being defended

Figure 3.6 With the ball in the possession of the right-hand attacking three, every defender marks the channel between themselves and the player on their right (or the side-line if they are a winger).

This drill allows the defenders to gain an understanding and a visual image of their positioning when the ball is in possession of each attacking three. Defenders should rotate positions to become familiar with the defensive demands of the wing, link and middle positions. The drill can be developed so that the attack can pass the ball to any of the attacking six, with the defenders again positioning themselves in response to which attacking three has the ball. It can be further developed to increase the pace at which the skills are being practised, the area in which it is taking place is increased, etc.

Shutting – the last resort

Earlier it was outlined how a defender is primarily responsible for marking a channel (rather than a specific attacker). Every attempt should be made by the individual defender to control the space they are defending so that they do not require the help of a defensive colleague. However, a defender may be beaten on either their outside or inside shoulder by an error in their own initial positioning, the pace of an attacker or the attacker's ability to shift the point of attack from one side of the defender to the other so quickly and effectively that the defender is taken out of the game. This may be accomplished through a side step or through the execution of an effective cut (a switch or 'scissors' move, which is discussed later from an attacking point of view). However it is brought about, if accomplished, it results in an overlap towards the side of the field which the ball-carrier is attacking. There is very little sympathy on offer for the defender who is beaten on their outside – this after all is the primary responsibility of a defender and good positioning keeps the likelihood of being beaten on the outside to a minimum. The following passage discusses how a defence can react to a defender being beaten on their inside.

In Figure 3.7, the attacking side has used the defence's care for their short side against them. The defenders' momentum is taking them towards the channel on their outside shoulder; this is the channel they should be defending when the ball is in the possession of a member of the attacking three on that side of the field. However, this momentum will take the defender away from the attacker if the ball-carrier cuts with the player on their outside. If the defender is beaten and cannot recover to make the touch they must call 'shut'. This informs their fellow defender on the inside that they must take responsibility for making the touch on the ball-carrier. On one level, the role of the shutting defender does not change – the ball-carrier is in the channel they are defending, so making the touch is their responsibility. However, even astute defenders can momentarily hesitate to step away from the player whom they were nominally marking in order to cover for a fellow defender. They must do so, as the alternative is to simply allow the attacker through the channel to score. The action of the defender leaving the attacker they were nominally marking to make the touch on the next player along is called a 'shut' as the defence is collectively 'shutting the door' on the space the attack has made vulnerable.

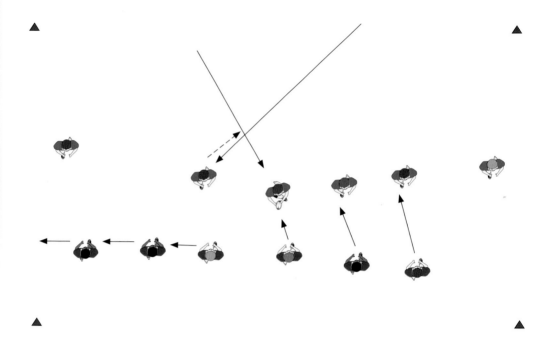

Figure 3.7 When the call of 'shut' comes, every defender on the inside of the beaten defender responds by leaving the player they were nominally marking and making the touch on the next attacker along.

A defender's hesitation at leaving the player they were nominally marking in order to make the touch is due to their understanding that the attacker they were initially marking will become free. To avoid the ball-carrier simply passing the ball to the next attacker and a try being scored one channel along, all the defenders must follow the shutting defender in also leaving the player they were nominally marking to make the touch on the next attacker along. Every defender on the side of the field that the attacker is stepping or cutting towards must respond in the manner above in order to pressurise the attack. Players must understand that the shut will leave the outermost attacker on the far side of the field free; however, it is relatively hard for the attacking side to get the ball into the outermost attacker's hands (through each player passing the ball down the line or through a long pass). It is therefore a calculated risk on the part of the defence and is an example of accepting that the attack may score having beaten a defender – but that the defence collectively will make the act of scoring as difficult as possible.

4 DEVELOPING ATTACKING PLAY

This chapter describes the roles and skill set required by the different positions in a touch team when in possession of the ball. It also explains how possession skills can be applied to a game of touch to achieve a performance advantage over the opposition. The following principles and patterns of play are intended to help a team develop a simple, straightforward tactical approach when attacking. Players and coaches can have confidence that if the following moves are executed effectively they will result in defenders being pulled out of position, creating space somewhere on the field. If space does not emerge at first, teams should develop their mastery of basic skills and their application, trusting that gaps in the defence will appear if the attackers' implementation of the following is consistently effective.

Position specific roles in attack

As teams develop their mastery of basic attacking skills and look to apply them to a game situation they will discover that specific demands are made of each position on the field. For example, all players are required to possess a good level of skill in passing and catching but some players may be better at jumping to catch the ball above defenders or have a greater level of skill in catching the ball as they dive towards the score-line. These abilities would be most effectively used on the wing rather than in the middle. The following briefly outlines the demands made of each position in an attacking context. It is helpful for players and coaches to know that some teams number the positions occupied by players on the field to help with on-field communication. The wings are number 1, the links number 2 and the middles number 3.

MIDDLE (3)

The middle is likely to handle the ball repeatedly and therefore needs to possess a high level of skill in passing and catching. They will also ruck the ball frequently; the ability to execute this core skill effectively is very important. The middle is likely to have a significant role in driving the ball up the field. Nearer the score-line, the middle has two players on their short side and three on their long side and they will have possession of the ball at an early stage in each phase of play. Therefore they have a greater range of options from which to choose about which side of the field to attack and to whom they will pass the ball, so the middle is often the player with the greatest ability to make correct decisions under pressure from the defence. When attacking the score-line, middles can create a number of attacking opportunities through rucking the ball and splitting wide (offering themselves as an option for the acting half to pass to) or through stepping and diving. Agility is an important quality. In addition, the middle is likely to be involved in a lot of second-phase play, that is, they are likely to be near the ruck created when a defence has shut down a phase of attacking play. Therefore the ability to throw a long pass to beat a defence that has moved infield to shut is beneficial.

LINK (2)

The link will have a major role in driving the ball up the field and needs to possess good rucking skills. Nearer the score-line the link is the attacker most likely to get the opportunity to exploit space on the outside of their defender. They are also the attacker most likely to receive an offloaded pass in executing a cut. Therefore pace is a very useful trait for a link to possess. Links and wings have a greater number of opportunities to attack space off second-phase play; they must develop the skill of reading the defence and hitting the correct side of the defender depending on the situation (outside their defender in an overlap; inside their defender in a 'man on' scenario). Passing and catching is an important characteristic of a link.

WING (1)

The wing can take pressure off the middles and links by coming infield to help drive the ball up the field. Nearer the score-line, wings and links have a greater number of opportunities to attack space off second-phase play; they must develop the skill of reading the defence and hitting the correct side of the defender (out to in if the defence is man on; staying outside their defender in an overlap). The wing will most often be in a position to receive a long pass from another attacking player so the ability to catch both high and low passes is important. Because the wing is most often in this position, they are often taller than links or middles.

Rucking in a game situation: the three-man drive

Gaining field position quickly and simply requires three players to execute the three-man drive. The first player initiates the touch and executes the roll ball, the second is the acting half and the third is the runner who receives the ball. This is the first phase of play. The acting half follows their pass and wraps around the runner they have passed to in anticipation of becoming the runner on the next phase of play; the runner who receives the ball will execute the next ruck by initiating the touch on the defender and rolling the ball; the player who executed the first ruck continues their forward momentum from the roll ball, advancing to become the acting half in the second phase of play.

In a game context, the three players are attempting to advance the ball up the field as effectively and quickly as possible. The runners will ideally run at and isolate a single defender so as to increase the chances of catching a defensive player offside. Each ruck is executed as efficiently as possible to lessen the amount of time the defence has to get organised. Reducing the amount of time the defence has to retreat and get into position can be achieved in two ways. One method is to ensure that the ball is stationary on the ground for as little time as possible. This is accomplished by the ball-carrier ensuring that they ruck the ball in front of the player who will be the acting half. If the ball-carrier receives the pass and they are some distance from the acting half it is their responsibility to 'find' the acting half, that is, angle towards them. The acting half will also look to shape and time their own movements to the ball-carrier in order to pass the ball from the ground as soon as possible. Another way to minimise the time the defence has to organise themselves is for runners to receive the pass from the acting half on the gain line (timing their run so as to receive a pass that has gone backwards from the acting half but which is as close to the lateral line of the roll ball as possible). The nomination of roles in the drive that rotate in the manner outlined above helps the attacking team to achieve both of these characteristics in their rucking.

Scooping

If driving is effective and a defender is caught offside within 15 metres of the score-line, the acting half may decide to scoop the ball off the deck without breaking their stride and run through the offside defender (if the defender touches the half it does not count as they were in an offside position). The half cannot score and if they are legally touched before they have passed the ball, possession will be immediately given to the defending side. However, with the half 'in behind' the defence, defensive organisation often falls apart; it is common for another defender to try to cover the offside defender and catch the scooper; but if they do so an attacker will have become free to pass to, enabling a simple score. Hard driving followed by a scoop is a straightforward way to score in touch; it is very hard to defend if effectively executed (even if the defence anticipates the attacking side's intention); and it is probably the most common scoring play. Teams should focus on getting this type of play right before they attempt to move on to anything more complicated.

DRILL 14

Create a 20-metre square using cones; a defender stands at cone C, a ball-carrier at cone B and their fellow attacker at cone A (as shown below). The ball-carrier accelerates forward to attack the space outside the defender, pulling the defender across the square towards cone D. The ball-carrier finds the acting half and initiates the touch on the defender; having executed the ruck they continue to move with their momentum to the side ready to receive a pass from the acting half. The defender should retreat five metres from the ruck and cover the space between themselves and cone D (into which the initial ball-carrier is splitting). The acting half scoops up the ball without breaking stride and accelerates into the channel between the defender and cone C.

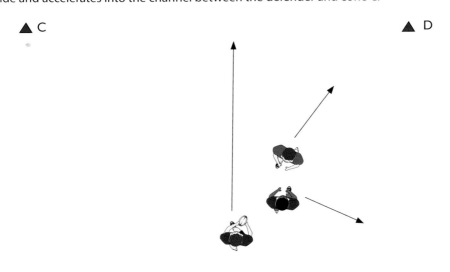

▲ C   ▲ D

▲ B   ▲ A

Figure 4.1 The acting half scoops, accelerating into the channel between the defender and the cone from which the defender has just moved while the initial ball-carrier splits out to the right-hand side of the square.

The aim of the drill is for the scooper to run decisively from acting half and into space. To develop the drill, two defenders stand opposite the ball-carrier; the second defender does not move from the cone and the scooper accelerates into the channel between the defender on whom the touch is initiated and the stationary defender. As a further development of the drill, the stationary defender is allowed to move but a third attacker joins the drill. The ball-carrier executes the ruck and the scooper attacks the channel between the two defenders. If the second defender closes down on the acting half the third attacker will be free for the scooper to pass to. If the second defender does not close down on the acting half then the scooper breaks through and runs over the score-line while the two unmarked attackers find space in which they receive the pass and score.

DRILL 15

Mark out a square approximately 30 metres wide and 30 metres long. Three attackers start with the ball at one end of the square and execute the three-man drive against three defenders. The attackers look to isolate one defender and initiate every ruck on this one player. When an opportunity presents itself the acting half scoops and attacks the shoulder of the defender on which there is more space while the other two attackers look to find a position in which they can be passed to and score.

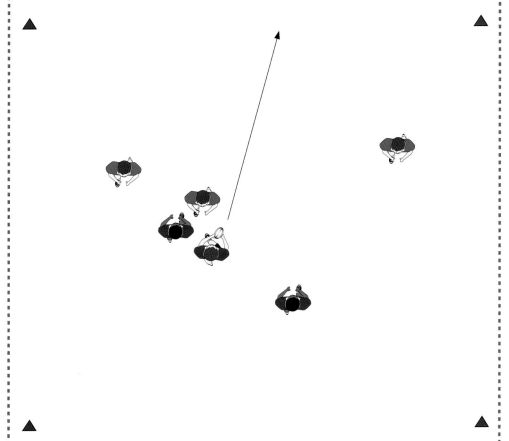

Figure 4.2 The three-man drive has isolated the middle defender and opened space between them and the defender on the right as the attackers look upfield. The acting half scoops, accelerating into the channel between the middle defender and the defender on the right.

Building on the drag-down

Many teams use the drag-down as a pattern of play when field position has been gained but the defence is not sufficiently disorganised to allow a scoop. A drag-down executed by the middle and the link is called a 32-down using the numbering system outlined earlier where the 3 is a middle and a 2 their nearest link. 'Down' refers to rucking the ball. While a single 32-down draws defenders to one side of the field – and thus opens up space for the attackers to exploit on the side of the pitch furthest from the ruck – it is unlikely to immediately create a scoring opportunity. Therefore there is much to be said for teams taking a simple starting pattern like a 32-down and creating a number of variations of it to increase its attacking potential. Such an approach gives all the attackers familiarity with how to initiate an attack, so if players are caught out of position or have subbed off, the attack will still flow. It also creates difficulties for the defence in reading precisely what the attack is going to do. When the attack performs a 32 near to the score-line the defence will be prepared for some sort of play, but will have to position themselves to cover a number of eventualities. For further discussion of building options on to a foundational attacking play with a variety of options leading from it read the Chapter 6 on tactical touch.

32s

A middle in possession of the ball engages their defender and attacks the channel on their outside shoulder. The link on their outside prepares to become the acting half. Having dragged their defender to the outside, the middle initiates the touch and rucks the ball before splitting to the outside. In this circumstance the acting half uses the splitting player

Figure 4.3 The right-hand middle and link have executed a 32, with the right-hand middle splitting to the outside. The acting half passes to the left-hand middle who looks to execute a 32 with their nearest link.

as a dummy option and passes away from the splitter to the middle on the other side of the field; they and their link execute the same play, passing the ball to the side of the field where the 32s began. This pattern is repeated until an opening emerges.

The repetition of 32s is designed to pull the defence from one side of the field to the other; if executed effectively, there will come a point where fatigue will lead to space opening up for attackers to exploit. However, this is a standard pattern that experienced sides are accustomed to defending, so even if it is executed effectively it may take several sets of six before openings appear.

SHORT

If a defence starts to anticipate repeated 32s, the attack may run a 'short' as an alternative play. Following a 32, the acting half passes away from the splitting attacker to the other middle whose initial position suggest that they will also execute a 32 or attack the outside of their defender. Instead the middle calls 'short' and steps infield to run on to a short pass in the space between the two middle defenders (with the intention of drawing both in to make the touch). The half follows their pass, wrapping or looping around the ball-carrier; if both defenders have been drawn in, the wrapping link will now be unmarked and a three-on-two will emerge on the opposite side of the field to where the ruck occurred.

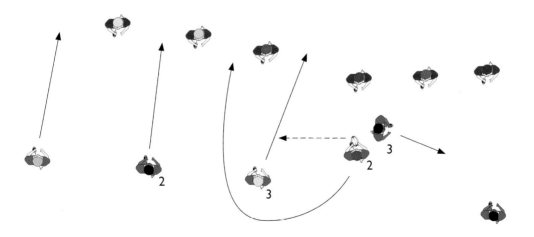

Figure 4.4 Executing a short.

LONG

If a defence starts to anticipate a short, the attack may run a 'long' as an alternative play. Following a 32, the middle who is due to receive the ball positions themselves as if they are going to attack the space between the two middle defenders (with the intention of keeping them from the far side of the field) and calls 'long'. Instead of a short pass between the two middle defenders, the half makes a long, flat pass to the outside of the furthest middle defender. As the half passes the ball, the middle receiving the pass makes a sharp change of direction to run on to the ball. With the initial positioning, the flat pass and the sharp change of direction, the middle receiving the ball is hoping to keep the defenders on the side of the field where the ruck occurred and exploit the space on the other side of the field.

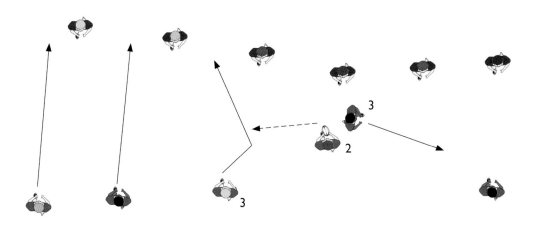

Figure 4.5 Executing a long.

BACKDOOR

Following a 32 (where a middle has rucked the ball and their outside link is the acting half), the winger nearest to the ruck undercuts it as it is being executed, looping or wrapping around the middle and link. They receive a short pass from the acting half on the inside of the ruck; they then straighten the angle of their run, accelerating into the channel of space between the two middle defenders (with the intention of drawing the middle furthest from them into making the touch). If the wing accelerates into the channel between the two middle defenders effectively, there will be a four-on-three on the opposite side of the field to where the ruck occurred.

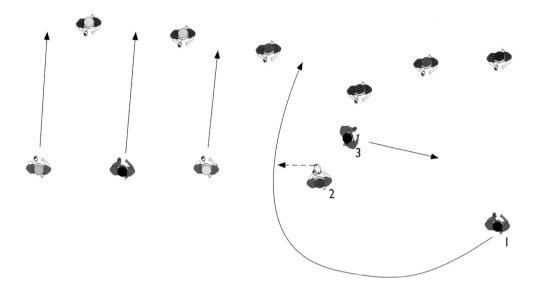

Figure 4.6 Executing a backdoor.

In a side where the playing positions are numbered, the winger who intends to run the backdoor might communicate to the middle and link nearest to them that they should run a '32, 1 backdoor'. However, 'backdoor' is the call adopted by any player to indicate that they are undercutting the ruck – it is not exclusive to a winger undercutting a ruck comprising of a middle and a link. A backdoor simply involves a player undercutting the ruck nearest to them, the purpose being to attack the opposite side of the field that was being attacked by the initial play. For example, it could be used by a link where the middle furthest from them has executed a 33 (a drag-down with the other middle); the link then undercuts the ruck, creating a three-on-two on the opposite side of the field from where the middle who performed the ruck is splitting.

Switching the point of attack (scissors, switch or cut)

The advantage of the cut (switch or scissors as it is called in rugby) is that it achieves all that a 32 does but saves a touch. Where the ball-carrier is a middle running a drag line and their nearest link realises that the chasing defender is not going to be beaten on their outside, the link communicates that they are going to 'cut' (that is, undercut the line run by the ball-carrier), receive the ball from them and attack the space on the inside shoulder of the chasing defender. This puts the defender in serious difficulties as they are already chasing to their outside to cover the ball-carrier's run.

To be effective the cut needs to be anticipated before the ball-carrier is in imminent danger of being touched. In the majority of cases the link will have a better view of the defence and will be better able to judge how hard the defender is chasing (the harder the defender is chasing, the more effective the cut will be) and the size of the gap between the chasing defender and their teammate on the inside. Therefore the decision to cut is primarily the link's. The ball-carrier should deliver the offloaded pass by turning through 180–270 degrees towards their outside, that is, they should continue to face the player they are delivering the pass to and as the receiver undercuts their run so that when the ball is passed both attackers have maintained eye contact. A cut can be a scoring move if the defender on the inside of the chasing defender has not followed their teammate quickly enough – in this circumstance the link that cuts can receive the ball and straighten into the space between the two defenders without being touched.

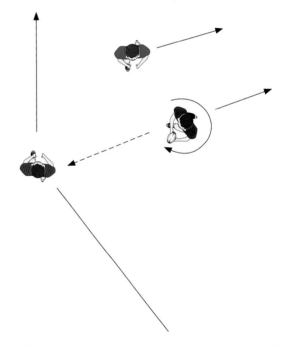

Figure 4.7 The ball-carrier attacks the space on one side of the defender before the cutting player attacks the space on the other side.

DRILL 16

Mark out two ten-metre (width) by 20-metre (length) rectangles next to each other; the ball-carrier stands at the bottom of rectangle A and their fellow attacker stands at the bottom of rectangle B. One defender stands opposite the ball-carrier approximately two-thirds of the way up rectangle A. The ball-carrier advances and attacks the side of the defender where there is space (the defender's outside shoulder), attempting to drag the defender from rectangle A to rectangle B. The attacker who is not carrying the ball remains standing out wide in rectangle B until the defender crosses from one rectangle to the other. At that point the attacker in rectangle B communicates that they are going to cut. They undercut the run of the ball-carrier, angling into rectangle A at which point they receive an offloaded pass from the ball-carrier. On receiving the ball, the attacker straightens and accelerates towards the line, where they score.

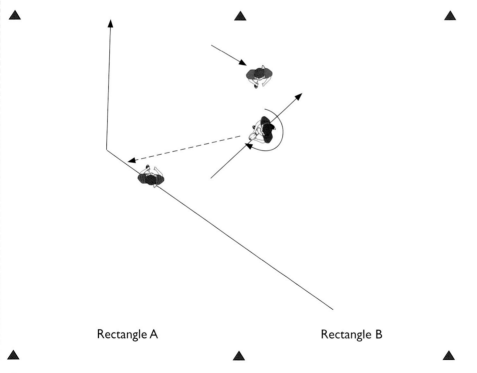

Rectangle A   Rectangle B

Figure 4.8 The ball-carrier moves the defender from one channel to another, creating space for the cutting player to accelerate into.

DRILL 17

Mark out a 20-metre by 20-metre square; have at least two players at each of the four corners of the square. The first player at cone B carries the ball; the first player at cone A acts as their fellow attacker. The first player at cone C marks the ball-carrier; the ball-carrier attacks the side of the defender where there is space (the outside shoulder of the defender). The ball-carrier attempts to drag the defender towards the side of the square marked by cones A and D. When the ball-carrier has committed the defender to chase hard across the square, the outside attacker sharply changes their direction and calls 'cut'. The ball-carrier continues their line of running and passes the ball while rotating to their left so

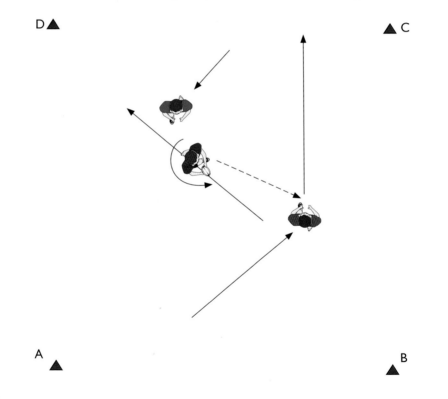

Figure 4.9 The ball-carrier attacks the left-hand side of the square where there is space; when the defender has moved across the square to cover the run of the ball-carrier the attacker cuts into the space left vacant by the defender.

that they are always able to see their fellow attacker (making the pass easier to deliver). If the defender has been dragged effectively then the receiver of the pass will be in space as they get the ball, at which point they straighten their line of running so that they are moving parallel to the sides of the square. They then pass the ball to the first player at cone C and join the queue at cone C. The other attacker and defender join the queue at cone D. The first two players at cones C and D repeat the drill coming back down the square with the first player at cone B acting as the defender. To practise the cut passing off the other hand, place the ball with the first player at cone A with the first player at cone D acting as the defender.

As a development of the drill – and to challenge the attackers – have the first two players on the cones at the opposite side to the attackers defend the cut. If the attackers do not perform it effectively enough, the chasing defender should leave the ball-carrier to his fellow defender and instead mark the cutting player. To keep the defenders working as in a game situation, encourage the attackers to play the situation rather than the drill, that is, if the defenders stand very narrow because they know a cut is coming, the attackers should simply put the ball through the hands to score on the outside; when the defenders stand wider to counter this possibility, the cut becomes a good option once again.

Building on the cut

A cut has to be executed very accurately if it is to be effective in the first phase of play. Attacking sides should look to use the cut in conjunction with the patterns of play already discussed in this section to increase its effectiveness.

LONG-CUT

Following a 32-down, the middle who is due to receive the ball calls 'long'. The execution of the long – the initial positioning, the flat pass and the sharp change of direction – all allow the middle receiving the ball to effectively attack the channel on their defender's outside. Consequently the defender chases very hard across the field, which in turn makes it more likely that the cut will be effective; the link on the ball-carrier's outside communicates that they are going to cut and they undercut the line run by the ball-carrier, receive the ball from them and attack the space on the inside shoulder of the chasing defender. This puts the defender in serious difficulties as they are already chasing hard to their outside.

SHORT-CUT

Following a 32-down, the middle who is due to receive the ball calls 'short'. If both middle defenders are drawn in to make the touch on the ball-carrier who is accelerating into the channel between them, the ball is passed to the wrapping link who is faced with a three-on-two on the opposite side of the field to where the ruck occurred. Consequently the defensive middle nearest to the wrapping link has to chase very hard across the field, which in turn makes it more likely that the cut will be effective; the link on the ball-carrier's outside communicates that they are going to cut and they undercut the line run by the ball-carrier, receive the ball from them and attack the space on the inside shoulder of the chasing defender. This puts the defender in serious difficulties as they are already chasing hard to their outside.

Developing angles of running

When the defence is 'man on' (there is no overlap), the only way attackers will meet with success in attacking the side of the defence where there are fewest defenders outside the engaged defender (the outside) is if they have a significant pace advantage over the player opposite them. If this advantage does not exist then running into this space without an overlap scenario can actually be helpful to the defence as the angle of the attacker's run is likely to close down the amount of space the defender needs to cover. For the wing defender, the side-line can act as a 'seventh defender' on the field as they usher the attacker towards it. In a 'man on' scenario the attackers are as likely to find as much space on the inside shoulder of the defender (the inside channel). This also has the advantage of going against what the defence might expect on the basis of the plays outlined so far.

RUNNING OUT-TO-IN

The potential receiver drifts towards the side of the defender nearest a side-line (the defender's outside), pulling the defender towards one side of the field. As the ball-carrier prepares to pass, the receiver changes their angle of movement and accelerates into the space on the side of the defender furthest from a side-line. The ball-carrier passes to the space – not the player – and the receiver attempts to dive, catch and score.

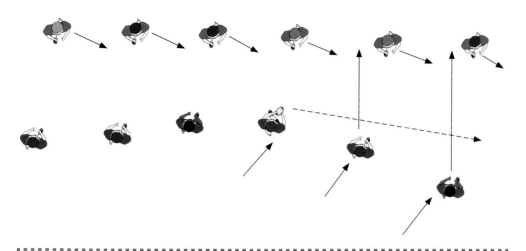

Figure 4.10 The outside-shoulder to inside-shoulder angle should be adopted by attackers when the defence is man on and there is little space on the defenders' outside shoulders.

GAME APPLICATION

The middle and link execute a cut. The link receives the offload and straightens into the channel between the two defensive middles; they then immediately pass the ball to the middle on their inside and get ready to become the acting half. The inside middle angles infield, drawing their defensive middle with them and initiates the touch on their defender as soon as they can and rucks the ball. The attackers outside the ruck drift towards the channel on the outside of their defender. As the acting half prepares to pass the ball off the ground, both players sharply change direction and accelerate into the channel on the inside of their defenders. The acting half decides in which channel there is more space and passes to that channel. Both receivers must therefore be anticipating the need to dive, catch and score.

DEVELOPING DEFENSIVE STRATEGY

This chapter describes the roles and skill set required by the different positions in a touch team when in defence and explores how a defending team can attempt to limit the performance advantage achieved by the attacking side. The following principles are intended to help a team develop a simple, straightforward tactical approach when defending. Players and coaches should keep in mind that the rules of touch favour the attacking side; but with thought and effective application of effort a team can become very difficult to score against.

Position specific roles in defence

MIDDLE (3)
The middle makes a large number of touches in defence. Attacks will often look to isolate the middle in driving plays and exploit their lateral movement near to the score-line. Endurance (to get up and back repeatedly in midfield) and agility to mark players on the line

are important traits for middles to possess. As in attack, the defensive middle will observe two attackers on one side of them and three on the other; they have the most options confronting them and the ability to read the game and the intentions of the attack is very useful. This is particularly the case with the middle who is not being directly engaged by the attack's play as they have the opportunity to anticipate which channel the attack is about to accelerate into and can position themselves accordingly. The earlier a middle can do this, the better for their team.

LINK (2)

The link's ability to defend their outside will be tested in defence, as will their ability to read the attack's intention to cut. If they can anticipate that the attacker they are defending is about to undercut the middle, the defensive link can work with their middle by marking the attacking middle and getting the defensive middle to mark the undercutting link. The defensive link will be put under a lot of pressure in a shut scenario near to the line; again, the ability to anticipate whether a shut is likely to be required and position themselves accordingly is required.

WING (1)

The defensive wing will be put under a lot of pressure in a shut scenario near to the line; it is most frequently the channel that the wing is shutting where an attacking side scores. A wing needs to possess the ability to anticipate whether a shut is likely to be required and position themselves accordingly. The wing will often be the defender over whom a long ball will be thrown and can therefore contribute to a team by reading when attacking teams are getting set to throw a long ball and make an interception. As in attack, height is a natural advantage for a winger, alongside great catching ability.

Defending the scoop

Defences are likely to face attacking sides attempting to ruck hard to get forward momentum and then scoop when the defence is in retreat and disorganised. The best way to defend against the scoop is to defend effectively in the midfield so that the defence is never rolling back and always organised so that the attack does not have the opportunity to scoop. However, if an acting half does scoop and gets in behind the defence, the defender who was nominally marking the player who is the acting half should chase down the scooper while the other defenders stay man on and mark the player opposite them. If another defender is nearer to the scooper they may communicate that they will undertake the chase, in which case the defender nominally marking the acting half must mark another attacker.

DRILL 18

On a full-width pitch about 15 metres out from the score-line they are defending, six defenders stand facing the line they are defending. One attacker stands next to the ball two or three metres in front of any defender of their choosing; they are the acting half. The other attackers stand behind the backs of the defenders in any formation or positioning they wish. On the coach's command, the acting half picks up the ball and accelerates towards the score-line. The defender standing directly behind the acting half chases down the scooper while the other defenders turn and attempt to mark the remaining attackers and attempt to prevent a score.

Score-line

Figure 5.1 A drill practising how to defend against an acting half scooping.

Reading the attack in order to stay man on

As outlined earlier, defenders should remain man on if at all possible and not require help from teammates to defend the space they are responsible for, as this will lead to space being opened up in other areas of the field. The majority of the time it will be obvious which attacker is the primary threat to a channel or area of space. However, touch is a fluid game and attackers will change positions on the field; when this occurs, the defender remains responsible for protecting the space in their defensive channel even if the specific attacker they were marking swaps positions with another player on the field.

The principle of each defender taking responsibility for their channel – along with an understanding of which channel defenders are responsible for – helps to give players some tools with which to counter attacking patterns of play. In Figure 5.2, the left middle (as the defence looks upfield at the attackers) has attacked the defender marking them on the side where the defender has fewest fellow defenders (the outside – in this case, on the defender's left). However, the defensive middle has effectively marked the channel on their left and it becomes clear that they are not going to be beaten on the outside. The attacking middle is touched and executes a ruck; they split out and become an option to pass to for the link nearest to them who has become the acting half. When the rucking player splits into the defensive link's channel and the acting half picks the ball up in the defensive middle's

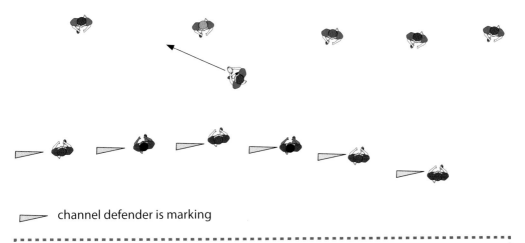

⊳ channel defender is marking

Figure 5.2 The left-hand defensive middle and link continue to mark the space outside their left shoulders irrespective of the fact that the player in that channel has changed.

channel, the two attackers have swapped positions – but that is not hugely relevant as the ball has stayed with the left-hand side attacking three. Therefore the defensive middle and defensive link hold their positions and continue to mark the channel between them and the player on their left, even though the specific player attacking that channel has changed.

In Figure 5.3 (below), the right middle (as the defence looks upfield at the attackers) has dragged across the field, attacking the defender marking them on their right-hand side where they have fewest fellow defenders. However, the right-hand side defensive middle has effectively marked the channel on their right and it becomes clear they are not going to be beaten on their outside. The ball-carrier executes a lazy cut with the link nearest to them, the link undercutting the run of the middle and receiving an offloaded pass. The two attackers have swapped positions – but that is not hugely relevant as the ball has stayed with the right-hand side attacking three. Therefore the defensive middle and defensive link hold their positions and continue to mark the channel between them and the player on their right, even though the specific player attacking that channel has changed.

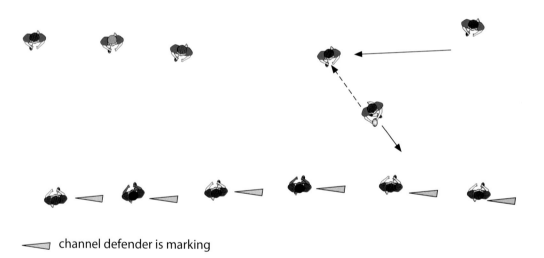

◁ channel defender is marking

Figure 5.3 The right-hand defensive middle and link continue to mark the space outside their right shoulders irrespective of the fact that the player attacking that channel has changed.

In both these examples, the defensive middle has marked their channel and not over-chased the player attacking it. However, if the defensive middle had been caught out of position in either circumstance and then had to chase down the ball-carrier, it would be very hard for them to make the touch and then hold their position as all of their momentum would be taking them to the outside of the pitch. In this circumstance, communication between the defensive middle and the link outside them is crucial. If either observes that the defensive middle's ability to mark their channel effectively is going to be compromised by over-chasing, the link should move infield as the middle makes the touch; the middle should then retreat five metres into the link position as the link marks the channel between themselves and the retreating middle if the ball remains in the possession of their attacking three.

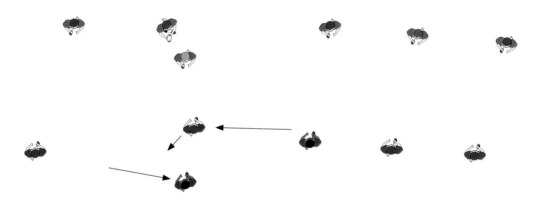

Figure 5.4 The left defensive link observes that the left defensive middle has chased hard to cover the space on their left-hand side and their momentum will take them further to the left. The defensive link moves infield as the defensive middle makes the touch and the defensive middle retreats to the link position. In effect the two players have swapped positions to deny the attacking team space.

It is important to note that if the defensive link moves infield before their middle has overcommitted, a large space appears in the link's channel that the attack can then exploit. The decision to move in must be the correct one and comes with experience (especially of specific players defending alongside each other as they start to read how well each other copes with certain situations). Defensive rotation is most commonly seen between the wing and the link as many sides try to limit the number of touches a winger makes. If wingers step infield unnecessarily to make touches, defences can be very vulnerable on that side of the field. Stepping in – particularly to make a touch on an attacker who is not playing on the wing – leaves space on the outside and gifts the attack an overlap for which it has not had to work. The link on the winger's inside should be aware of helping the winger avoid unnecessary defensive work. If the defensive link has to chase their own player into a wide position – or they have chased out hard to protect their short side and the ball has then been passed to the attacking winger – they would find it hard to make the touch and then hold their position (as all of their momentum would be taking them to the outside of the pitch). These circumstances lend themselves to the wing moving infield as the link makes the touch and the link retreating five metres into the wing position. Thus the short side is defended, the wing does not do unnecessary defensive work and the link is not required to put great pressure on their body by working against its natural momentum to hold their defensive position.

DRILL 19

Mark out a 20-metre square. Place a cone at ten metres on both ends of the square so that two ten-metre channels – zones A and B – are visible within the playing area. Two attackers will run against two defenders. The ball-carrier (imagining they are the right-hand link) stands in zone A – a defender stands opposite, approximately five metres in front of the score-line they are defending. The ball-carrier attempts to drag the defender (who imagines they are the left-hand defensive link) from zone A into zone B. The defender attempts to make the touch on the ball-carrier before they have been dragged too far across the field. A second attacker (imagining they are the

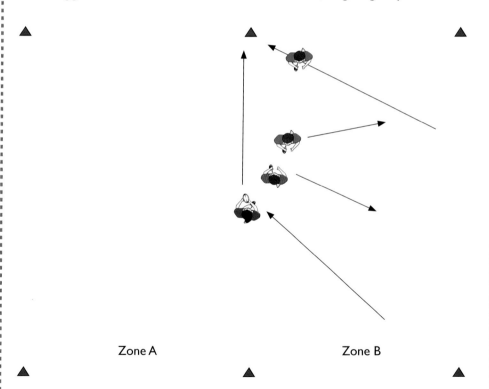

Zone A   Zone B

Figure 5.5 In this example the defender is chasing too hard to hold their position and the defender on their left-hand side moves infield as the touch is being made, swapping defensive positions with the engaged defender who retreats using their momentum from the chase.

winger) starts in zone B; a defender stands opposite them. The attacker stands in a wide position to keep the defensive wing in a wide position. When the ball-carrier has been touched and executed the ruck, they split with their momentum to the right-hand side of the field. The attacking wing becomes the acting half. They will pick the ball up and run straight towards the score-line. The defender who made the touch (imagining four more defenders to their right) communicates with the defender on their outside as to whether the chasing defender will be able to retreat five metres and effectively mark the channel attacked by the acting half after chasing in the manner dictated by the ball-carrier. If they are, the defenders retreat as normal; if not, as the chasing defender is making the touch the outside defender moves infield to mark the channel the acting half will run into while telling the chasing defender to 'stay out'. The options for the attackers are always the same – a scoop and driving run from the half or feeding the splitting player who executed the ruck. The attackers and defenders then swap roles.

This drill is about developing judgement – competitive match experience is invaluable but may not put defenders consistently in a position of having to make this kind of judgement, so training must perform this role instead. It also enables two players who are likely to play alongside each other in defence to get to know each other's capabilities and to develop effective communication with each other. Again, the demands of a competitive match are likely to see players pulled out of position at points, whereas training can create a consistent framework for developing understanding. While the attackers' options having rucked the ball are always the same, if the outside defender drifts in too early before the touch, the attackers should look to put the ball through the hands and attack the channel that has opened up (as they would do in a game).

Defending near the score-line

If one defender goes into the five-metre zone of the score-line they are defending then the whole team must advance forwards until the next touch in the set is 'imminent' in the referee's judgement. This prevents defenders simply hanging on their score-line (and consequently not having to retreat five metres or to the score-line once a touch has been affected as they are already in position). If the referee determines that a defender is not moving forward until the next touch is 'imminent' they will award a penalty against the defending team. If attacking sides have no momentum approaching the line then they may slow play down near to the line as they seek to pull the defence out, away from the line with the intention of causing them then to retreat at an angle that opens up space for the attackers to accelerate into.

Having made the touch near the line, the defender may choose any angle by which to retreat five metres but once they have begun retreating along that plane of movement they must retreat five metres before they can influence play. If the referee judges that the attacking side has been influenced by a player in an offside position, a penalty will be awarded against the defence. The defender should therefore aim to make the touch with their inside hand with their body angled outwards towards the short side when they are defending close to their line so they can turn and chase out hard if needs be or watch the attackers and turn to sprint and follow if the attacking side changes the point of attack.

Anticipating the shut

Reacting to the actions of an attacking side is difficult. If an attacker and defender have similar physical capabilities then the attacker has the advantage because they have the initiative. Therefore defenders must anticipate the need for the shut. Defenders should be taught that the shut is merely an application of the principle they are already familiar with – that they are responsible for defending the channel between themselves and the defender next to them who is nearest the ball-carrier. Shutting may feel different as defenders are stepping away from the attacker whom they anticipated marking. However, as it is the same principle as normal defending, anticipating the shut is a mental state and about awareness rather than a difference in positioning. As players become more experienced generally, or have specific experience working alongside a particular defender or against a particular attacker, they may start to anticipate what is about to happen sooner and be able to adjust their positioning accordingly.

DRILL 20

In an area 40 metres wide and approximately ten metres deep (from the score-line out past the five-metre line), four defenders line up against six attackers. The ball is carried by either the second attacker in from the left or the second attacker in from the right. The ball-carrier attacks the outermost defender on the side where there are no fellow defenders; the defender chases out to protect their short side. The ball-carrier executes a cut with the outermost attacker on that side; the chasing defender makes a judgement as to whether they can effectively close the channel that has been opened up. This judgement must be immediate and if it is in the negative the defender will call 'shut'. At the call of 'shut' all the defenders step in, leaving the attacker whom they were nominally marking to make the touch on the next attacker along who is nearer to the ball.

Score Zone

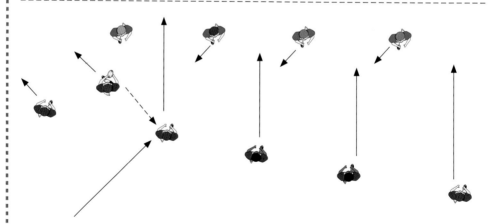

Figure 5.6 In this case the ball-carrier has caused the defender to chase too hard to be able to cover the cutting player. The chasing defender calls 'shut' and the defenders on their inside leave the players they were nominally marking to make the touch on the next attacker along towards the ball.

While primarily a defensive drill, the ball-carrier can ensure that the defender properly protects the outside channel by running hard and passing the ball to the outside attacker if the defender does not follow. Assuming the first defender has chased hard and the cut has been effective, the ball-carrier should play the options as they open up in front of them. If they are not shut down they should accelerate through the channel they are attacking to score; if they are shut down but one of the defenders responds late to the call of 'shut', the ball-carrier should identify which attacker is in space and pass the ball directly to them. Attacking sides often find that while the first shutting defender executes the policy effectively, each defender along the line tends to be less effective, resulting in the second or third attacker being in space. If all the defenders have anticipated the shut and have stepped in to close their channels, the furthest attacker on the outside will be in space and the ball-carrier should practice their ability to throw a long pass to this player. The drill outlined above can be developed simply by removing the starting pattern of a drag-cut and playing five attackers versus four defenders; this encourages both sets of players to read the game as it unfolds. The drill can be further developed by having six attackers playing against five defenders on a full-width field.

Defending against second phase

If a defence looks to operate a shut policy then attacking sides will ultimately look to use it against them. While the shut – if executed correctly – is highly effective in closing down a phase of play where a defender has been beaten, it does leave the defending team vulnerable on the side of the field from which they have shut. On this side of the field there is an overlap and the defenders are moving infield, away from the outside attacker. Therefore, having shut, the defenders now must move against their infield momentum to chase to the outside to try and prevent a score. Having shut, the defence has closed an easier opportunity for the attack to score than the opportunity they have opened up – but it has nonetheless presented the attack with a chance to score. The defence can now only put their hope on scramble defence creating enough pressure to induce an error by the attacking side.

DRILL 21

As a development of the drill for anticipating the shut, in an area 50 metres wide and approximately 15 metres deep (from the score-line out past the five-metre line), five defenders line up against six attackers. The attackers are not allowed to score off the first phase of play – they must execute a pattern that will result in the defence shutting (for example, cut or short). The defence shuts and then retreats five metres towards the side of the field exposed by the shut. The attack plays to exploit the opportunity it has been presented with.

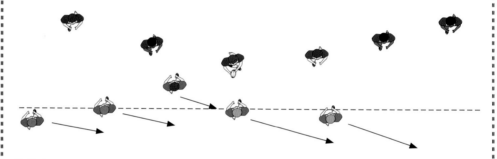

Score Zone

Figure 5.7 In this case the attacking middle and link on the left-hand side (as the defence looks upfield) have cut; the defensive middle could not cover the cutting player and the defence's right-hand link and wing shut successfully. All the defenders are now chasing out to their right-hand side to protect this space from the overlap.

To shut and then chase out is very difficult to accomplish effectively; the difficulty is enhanced in this drill by the defence being a man down. The rules of the drill regulating the actions of the attacking side are to ensure that the attack runs a play that in a game situation would be most likely to cause the defence to shut; and the defence being a player short makes it highly likely that a shut will be executed. The drill develops the shut-chase capabilities of the defence but also illustrates that the shut creates vulnerability in the defence and so is best avoided if at all possible.

6

PLAYING AT A HIGHER LEVEL – ATTACK

Like many sports, touch is essentially a straightforward game. As individuals and teams move from social games and local leagues to top club grade, regional level and international touch, they discover that teams are still simply trying to stretch a defence to make space in which to score. However, the simple skills discussed so far are executed correctly with greater consistency, at greater speed and with greater resistance to pressure from the defence the further up the performance tree one participates. While high performance teams use the same simple touch building blocks as everyone else, this chapter demonstrates how teams with mastery and consistent execution of basic skills can build a tactical approach to their attack. The way in which these teams play often looks complicated to an inexperienced eye, but that is simply the effect of observing a number of simple concepts executed skilfully and with pace in quick succession. At the highest level, teams may also take a principle of attack previously discussed and change simple aspects of it to create new variations and challenges for a defence; again, this may look more complicated than it really is. In addition, teams at a higher level are more likely to attack in phases (a 'phase' coming to a close as a touch is made and a ruck effected; so the first phase of play comes to a close with the first touch, the second phase with the second touch, etc.). Therefore the ambition of some of the early phases of a particular attacking approach will be to make the defence respond in a particular manner in order to exploit that behaviour and movement in a following phase of play.

Developing driving and rucking from the defensive line

Field position is important; the more possession a team has near to the score-line they are attacking, the higher their chance of scoring. If a team gains possession of the ball in the opponents' half of the field they have the option of executing an attacking play or strike move. However, if possession is gained near to the score-line a team is defending their priority is to advance the ball as far upfield as possible using the fewest touches. The three-man drive can be used; the following are alternative options (although based on the same principles of players running aggressively, rucking the ball in front of their acting half and with the ball on the ground for the least possible amount of time).

Often turnovers occur on the flanks out wide. At a more technical level of touch this can be caused deliberately by the team losing possession of the ball in an attempt to influence whether the team gaining possession will be advancing up the left- or right-hand side of the field in order to organise their defence accordingly. Some teams will go as far as to throw a speculative long ball deliberately out of the reach of their winger so that the ball has to be retrieved before the opposition's set of possession begins, gaining them time to organise their defence. This is illegal under the laws – but teams try it anyway. Driving up the middle of the field has the advantage of attacking (and potentially fatiguing) the opposition's middles, limiting their capacity to carry out their other defensive duties as effectively as they might and reducing the effectiveness of their attacking capabilities. It also gives the attacking side the option of probing the left- or right-hand side of the pitch when field position has been achieved. Coaches and players should therefore consider how they can transform a turnover on a defensive flank into a driving play up the middle of the field.

MIDFIELD RUCK—ONE OUTSIDE—ONE INSIDE

The two players nearest the turnover execute the ruck; one steps over the ball and the other is the acting half. The ball is passed down the line to the middle furthest from the ruck. They advance up the field and initiate the touch on their defender. The other middle becomes the acting half. Having executed the ruck, the ball-carrying middle holds their lateral position while moving up the pitch to become the acting half in the next phase of play. The acting half passes the ball to the link on the outside and wraps out to the wing, with the wing moving in to the link position. The link attacks the same defender who made the first touch, angling their run towards the nominated acting half (the middle who executed the original ruck). Having executed the ruck, the link holds their lateral position while moving up the pitch to become the acting half in the next phase of play. The acting half passes the ball to the link on the opposite side of the field and wraps out to the wing, with the wing moving in to the link position. The link attacks the same defender, angling their run towards the nominated acting half (the middle who executed the original ruck). If the drive has been executed effectively the defence – particularly the defender on whom the drive has been concentrated – will be struggling to stay onside. The defence may be vulnerable to the half scooping and, as the simplest option, this is preferable; alternatively, the attack may decide to set up a specific attacking move having achieved good field position. As well as advancing the ball and attacking the middles, this driving pattern has the advantage of rolling the links and wings into midfield. This is particularly helpful if a player has become stuck in an outside position in defence but wishes to become involved in the centre of the field in attack.

MIDFIELD RUCK—ONE OUTSIDE—TWO INSIDE

The two players nearest the turnover execute the ruck; one steps over the ball and the other is the acting half. The ball is passed to the middle furthest from the initial ruck who advances upfield and initiates the touch on their defender. The other middle becomes the acting half. Having executed the ruck the ball-carrying middle holds their lateral position while moving up the pitch to become the acting half in the next phase of play. The acting half passes the ball to the link on the outside and wraps out to the wing, with the wing moving in to the link position. The link attacks the same defender who made the first touch, angling their run towards the nominated acting half (the middle who executed the original ruck). Having executed the ruck, the link holds their lateral position while moving up the pitch to become the acting half in the next phase of play. The acting half passes the ball to the link on the opposite side of the field and wraps out to the wing, with the wing moving in to the link position. The link attacks the same defender, angling their run towards the nominated acting half (the middle who executed the original ruck). Having executed the ruck, the link holds their lateral position while moving up the pitch to become the acting half in the next phase of play. The acting half passes the ball to the player occupying the link position on the same side of the field as on the previous phase of play. The acting half wraps out to the wing, with the wing moving in to the link position. The ball-carrier attacks the same defender, angling their run towards the nominated acting half. If the drive has been executed effectively then the defence – particularly the defender on whom the drive has been concentrated – will be struggling to stay onside. The defence may be vulnerable to the half scooping and, as the simplest option, this is preferable; alternatively, the attack may decide to set up a specific attacking move having achieved good field position. As with the previous pattern, this drive has the advantage of rolling the links and wings into midfield. It does, however, use an extra touch, which can be a limiting factor on what the attack is able to accomplish when it gains the field position it is trying to achieve.

Scooping effectively

For the scoop to be effective, the acting half must be decisive; as the pass from the floor and the scoop require specific feet and body positioning, the acting half needs to be clear in their own mind what they are about to do as they approach the ball; picking the ball up and only then deciding what to do is much less effective. The player scooping should also know what they are looking to accomplish by doing so. If the ruck from which they are scooping is in the middle of the field and the ball is being rolled behind the defender, scooping will put the acting half in behind the defence. The defenders will chase back and it is likely that another defender will help out their beaten colleague to make the touch. Therefore the scooping player should pick up the ball and run hard and straight to ensure that they do get behind the defence and to make it more likely that a defender will leave the player they were initially marking to chase them down. As the scooping player reaches the score-line they will look to pass to the free attacker whose best chance of finding space is either out wide or in the hole immediately behind the scooper (where the scooper passed over the score-line). If the scooping player does not at first see a player who is free to pass to then they should run along the dead ball line towards a corner of the field to maximise their time on the ball. The other attackers should look to beat their defenders off the ball and cross the score-line in space in order to receive a pass. There should always be an attacker on the wing ready to receive a pass.

If a defensive middle makes the touch that leads to a ruck and the defence is moving to protect the short side, scooping can create an overlap on the long side. The scooping player should accelerate into the channel on the inside shoulder of the defender making the touch while the attackers on the long side accelerate into the channel on the outside shoulder of the defender nominally marking them. If the defence does not shut down the scooping player, they will be in behind the defence. If the defenders do look to shut, the ball should be put through the hands to exploit the overlap created.

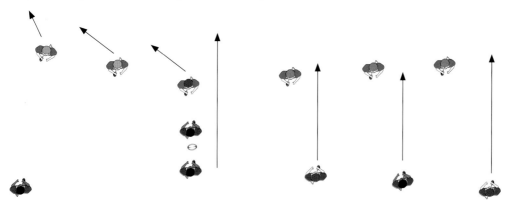

Figure 6.1 In this case the left-hand attacking middle has dragged across the field and rucked the ball. The defenders on the left-hand side of the field (as the attack looks upfield) are moving to protect the short side. The acting half scoops between the two middles while the attackers on the right-hand side of the field run outside their defenders. If the defenders stay with the right-hand attackers, the acting half will get through; if they step in, an overlap is created on the right.

If the defence effects a touch on one of the attackers (other than the acting half) and the ball is rucked, there is still an overlap on the side of the field where the defender made the touch and the half at this ruck may decide to scoop to the short side to draw in the defender/s before passing to exploit the mismatch of numbers.

Using the ball to stretch a defence

If a team has possession of the ball in the attacking half of the field but no momentum with which to ruck and scoop, the ball can be used to stretch the defence. To do so teams must have confidence in the basic skill set of their players; they need to be confident that they can look to attack space on one side of the field and – on finding that the space has been closed off – transfer the ball to the far side of the field to look for an alternative opportunity. The wider the ball can be spread, the bigger the space the defenders have to cover and the more fatigued they will become over the course of a game. Attacking the outside channels can be a useful tactic for an attacking team, using the link and wing in the hunt for space. If there is no space, the link or wing can always pass the ball inside (one pass if the link has possession or a miss-pass if the wing has possession) to the middle and set up one of the attacking plays discussed later in the chapter. If the middle ultimately receives the ball and sets up one of these plays, the preceding ball movement will have made the defenders move a long way across the pitch to cover it, opening up the far side of the field to the attackers.

Ideally, the wing is rarely touched in possession of the ball. If they are, the link has to move outfield to become the acting half leading to greater downtime on the ball. Additionally, the defence knows the direction that the ball will be passed as all the attackers will be on one side of the ruck. While it is not always avoidable, if the wing anticipates being touched they can simply pass the ball inside to the link; if they are touched the wing becomes the acting half having followed their pass (reducing the amount of time the ball is on the ground).

Rucking near the attacking score-line

If the attacking team has not been able to drive effectively enough to catch a defender offside then the scoop will not be a feasible option as there is a very good chance the half will be touched before they have passed the ball, turning over possession. A team may find itself in a position close to the score-line they are attacking but without momentum (for example, against a defence that is set). In these circumstances, rucking technique should be adapted to try and create opportunities to score. The primary aim of the ruck in these circumstances is not to advance the ball up the field as quickly as possible (as outlined earlier); instead players aim to use the ruck as a platform to generate quick ball and lateral movement to attack the space at the side of the defenders.

Players still need to be mindful of 'going over the mark', 'loss of control' and 'ball to ground'. Therefore they should still look to initiate the touch (to anticipate and control where they will have to ruck the ball). Attacking players should still attempt to ruck the ball to the side of the defender (to make retreating to an onside position as difficult as possible) and adopt a wide, strong stance with the legs. However, to generate significant lateral movement, some adjustment to technique is needed. Players should look to 'split' hard off the ruck, that is, attempt to make a significant, dynamic sideways movement as soon as they have placed the ball on the ground. Therefore the ball-carrier cannot carry significant forward momentum into the ruck as this would make 'splitting' hard very difficult, if not impossible. In addition, the front foot of the wide, strong stance is now also the push off foot for the split. Therefore it needs to be placed very carefully and players are likely to bend the knee more to create the required force to split hard. Players should now bear in mind that if they wish to split to their right they will need to initiate the touch on the defender with their left hand, left foot forward, placing the ball with their right hand, anticipating to spring to their right off their left leg; conversely, if a player wishes to split to their left they will need to initiate the touch with their right hand, right foot forward, placing the ball with their left hand, anticipating to spring to their left off their right leg.

Figure 6.2 Technique to adopt when rucking near the score-line in order to split to the left. (a) The rucking player initiates the touch with his right hand, right leg forwards;

(b) he 'splits' hard to his left;

(c) and receives the ball immediately from the acting half in space outside his defender.

Figure 6.3 Technique to adopt when rucking near the score-line in order to split to the right.
(a) The rucking player initiates the touch with his left hand, left leg forwards;

(b) he 'splits' hard to his right;

(c) and receives the ball immediately from the acting half in space outside his defender.

DRILL 22

Place two cones ten metres apart. Place another cone halfway between them and one metre in front of them. A ball-carrier should approach the central cone from a distance of seven to eight metres and practice the technique outlined above, placing the ball at the middle cone and alternately splitting sideways and back to the cone on the right and splitting sideways and back to the cone on the left. The slight backwards motion is to enable the splitting player to be in a position to receive a pass from the half as soon as possible.

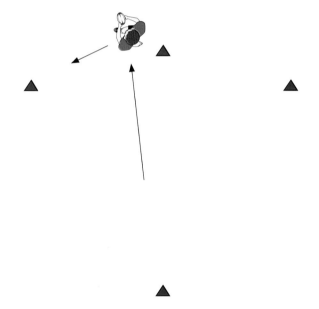

Figure 6.4 In this case the attacker has rucked the ball and split to their left.

As a development of the drill, have two attackers approach the central cone (a ball-carrier and an acting half). Once the ball-carrier has placed the ball on the floor, the half passes either left or right, depending on the direction that the ball-carrier is splitting. The aim should be for the ball to be on the ground for a maximum of one second and for the ball-carrier to split dynamically so that as they catch the pass from the half they are on the outside of the cone on the side they are splitting to. This is commonly known as a 'quickie'.

DRILL 23

Create a ten-metre square with the two attackers versus one defender. The defender must advance off the score-line. The ball-carrier should look to initiate the touch at a minimum of five metres away from the score-line (in order to make the defender retreat the maximum distance) and split to the side, aiming to receive the pass from the half and score before the defender can retreat five metres and make the touch. The defender must ensure that they retreat the full five metres to the score-line before they make the touch; they may retreat at an angle to attempt to cover the attacker's split.

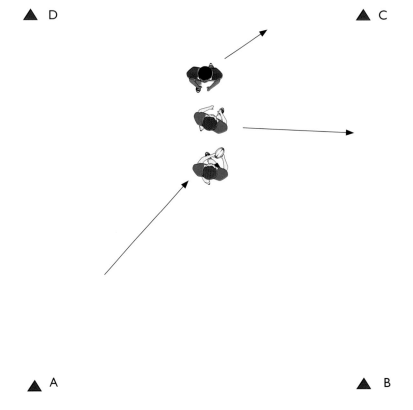

Figure 6.5 In this example the ball-carrier approaches from cone A and the defender from cone D. The attacker initiates the touch and splits to their right and the defender retreats at an angle to cover them. The acting half approaches from cone B and feeds the splitting player the ball.

Development of switching the point of attack

As indicated earlier the cut is most effective when the defender, whose inside shoulder the cutting player ends up attacking, is chasing hard to their outside. The cutting attacker's cue is what happens to the defender's hips; once the defender's hips have turned away from the channel on their inside there is very little possibility of them being able to cover this space once the cut has been effected. The cutting player should also make a calculation as to whether the next defender on the inside will be in a position to shut down the channel they will accelerate into when they receive the offloaded pass from their attacking colleague. If this defender is positioned poorly then it is possible that the cutting player will be able to straighten into the gap and accelerate through the defensive line to score. If the cutting player recognises that the defender is likely to shut the channel and make the touch on them, they should look to initiate the touch and set up another phase of play.

CUT-SECOND PHASE

In this pattern the attacking side is not primarily looking to beat the defence with a cut; instead they are looking to trigger the defensive shut and create a second phase of play. The attacking middle and link execute a cut. The link receives the offload and straightens into the channel between the two defensive middles; they then immediately pass the ball infield to the other middle and get ready to become the acting half. The inside middle angles towards the player who passed the ball, drawing the opponent marking them infield. They initiate the touch as soon as they can and ruck the ball. The acting half scoops the ball and accelerates into the channel on the side of the defender making the touch where they have fewest fellow defenders. The acting half may break through the line of defence or draw the next defender towards the outside and exploit the overlap.

Defenders may start to anticipate attackers performing a cut if it has been used on a number of occasions. If the cut is being performed by the attacking middle and their outside link, the defensive link may stop following the run of the attacking link and engage with the attacking middle, while the defensive middle may stop following the run of the attacking middle and look for the undercutting run of the attacking link. If a cut is executed in these circumstances, it will be ineffective – the cutting link will step straight into the defensive middle. The following patterns attempt to manipulate the defence if it starts to behave in this manner, manipulating the inward movement of the defenders.

Figure 6.6 In this example the right-hand middle is about to be touched. This follows the attacking left-hand middle (3) and link (2) having executed a cut and the link passing to the middle on their right, angling in. Following the ruck shown here, the link who performed the initial cut becomes the acting half and scoops to the right of the defender who made the touch.

DUMMY CUT (D-CUT)

In this pattern the attacking side is looking to make the defence expect a cut and accordingly anticipate the need to cover the side of the field on the inside of the ball-carrier. In reality the attacking side is going to attack the space outside the ball-carrier (a space that the attack is trying to make bigger by getting the defence to move infield or at least not to chase outfield). The ball-carrier attacks the outside shoulder of their defender and the player outside them shapes as if to undercut their run. On realising that the defenders are reacting to the cut – even though it has not been executed – the attacking middle and link communicate 'D-cut'. The link immediately steps back out to attack the space outside the defending link with the ball-carrying middle continuing to attack the outside shoulder of the defensive middle. If the defensive link is late in covering the run of the attacking link, the ball-carrying middle passes the ball and the link will break the defensive line and possibly score. If the defensive link covers the run of the attacking link but the defensive middle doesn't cover the run of the attacking middle, the middle keeps hold of the ball, breaking the defensive line, and will possibly score. If the runs of both the attackers are covered, the attackers will execute a drag-down (32) but, having made the defenders chase hard, opening up space on the opposite side of the field.

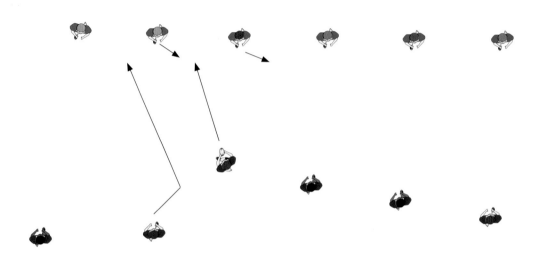

Figure 6.7 The attacking left-hand middle attacks the side of their defender where there are fewest fellow defenders. The attacking left-hand link angles in as if to cut; the defensive middle and link marking these two players shape infield, anticipating where they will end up. The link sharply changes direction towards the outside of the field, hoping to catch their defender flat-footed.

LAZY CUT/SWITCH, STEP BACK OUT

The ball-carrying middle and their nearest link (having observed the defence's expectation of a cut or switch) execute a shallow angled cut with the link moving more laterally and with less forward momentum than is normal. The cut is executed at about 60 per cent speed. Having offloaded the ball, the middle continues on the same lateral line; having received the ball, the link continues on their lateral line of movement infield for two or three strides, further encouraging the defenders to step infield. The ball-carrier then steps sharply back out, accelerating into the channel between the defensive middle and link; the attacking player who offloaded the ball accelerates sharply into the channel between the defensive link and the defensive wing.

The intention of this pattern is to push the defence infield and to catch the defenders flat-footed. If the defensive middle does not close the gap, the ball-carrier will break the defensive line and may score. If the defensive middle closes the gap but the defensive link does not, the ball-carrier will pass the ball out to the player who initiated the lazy cut who will break the defensive line and may score. If both defenders react quickly enough to

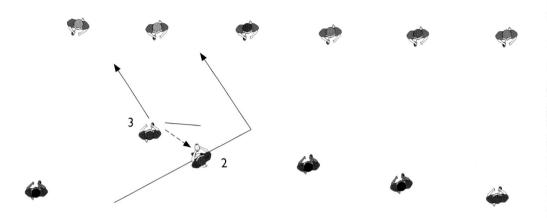

Figure 6.8 In this example the attacking left-hand middle (3) has drifted across field to their nearest link (2) and performed a shallow cut with them; having offloaded the ball they have continued on the same plane of movement for a few strides. The 2 has drifted infield causing the defensive link and middle opposite them to step infield. The 2 has then sharply accelerated back out; the 3 has mirrored their angle of run, catching the defence flat-footed.

close the channels being attacked, the attackers will execute a drag-down (32) but, having made the defenders chase harder than they expected to cover the move and unexpected acceleration, opening up space on the far side of the field.

LAZY SWITCH, ONE PASS, DOWN, BACKDOOR WRAP

As an alternative to the above, the middle performs a lazy switch with their nearest link. Having offloaded the ball, the middle continues on the same lateral line for two or three paces; having received the ball, the link continues along their lateral line and almost immediately feeds a pass to the inside middle (while preparing to become the acting half). The inside middle initiates the touch on their defender in order to ruck the ball, angling in as they do so. The lazy switch and the run of the middle who rucks the ball have the effect of bringing the two middle defenders together (and therefore marking the same space). The acting half looks to scoop on the outside shoulder of the defender on whom the touch has just been initiated. Meanwhile, the attacking player who offloaded the ball steps back against their momentum towards the side of the field they started on, sweeping around the ruck (backdoor) and straightening into the channel between the defensive middle and link. This creates an attacking overlap on the opposite side of the field to where the lazy switch was first performed.

Figure 6.9 (a) The middle and link have performed a lazy cut against their momentum and the ball-receiver drifts infield while looking as if she might return the pass;

(b) the ball-carrier in fact passes to the player on her inside while the original middle steps back;

(c) the infield middle initiates the touch and rucks the ball as the original middle sweeps underneath the ruck;

(d) the initial middle who performed the lazy cut becomes an extra attacker on the far side of the field.

Building on the backdoor

A backdoor is itself not likely to lead to a decisive break. However, if the phase before the backdoor has the effect of pulling the defenders away from the space into which the backdoor runner will accelerate then it is likely to be more successful. The backdoor will move defenders, which attacking teams can use to their advantage in the phase following it if it is not decisive.

MISS-PASS-BACKDOOR

This is not a typical backdoor move as it is not the player who undercuts the ruck but the ruck that overcuts the player. A link in possession of the ball delivers a miss-pass infield to the middle who is furthest away from them. The middle receiving the pass angles infield to initiate the touch on their defensive middle, pulling them infield and away from the short side. The link who delivered the miss-pass becomes the acting half and the middle who was missed by the pass undercuts the ruck to attack the short side, creating an overlap.

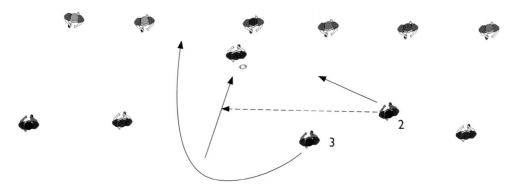

Figure 6.12 The link (2) delivers a miss-pass to the far middle who moves infield to initiate the touch and ruck the ball. The link follows their pass to become the acting half while the middle (3) who was missed by the pass wraps around the back of the ruck to create an overlap on the left-hand side of the field.

The overlap is created by the receiver of the miss-pass angling infield and the player missed by the pass attacking the channel on the outside of the defensive middle being drawn in by the ruck. The more the ruck overcuts the player, the more effectively space is opened up as the defender who was nominally marking the player running the backdoor is blocked off by their own defensive middle who is making the touch.

Multiple attacking variations on a theme

High-level defences will contain players who are familiar with reading what an attack may attempt to accomplish in certain circumstances. For example, teams that attack the channel outside the defensive middles but are clearly not about to initiate the touch can only be looking to beat the man on the outside or drag the middles apart to affect a cut. High-level attacks are therefore likely to formulate a starter move or starter pattern, with the capacity to then execute a variety of different options following it depending on the choices defenders start to make.

PLAYS ROOTED IN 32s

The pattern underpinning the following options involves a middle (3) executing a drag-down with their outside link (2) and splitting out once they have initiated the touch and rucked the ball (moving with their momentum).

Option 1

The middle executes a drag-down with the link and splits out; the link (as acting half) scoops, attacking the channel between the two defensive middles with the intention of breaking the defensive line without being touched or of running the line to effectively create a four-on-three on the other side of the field to where the ruck occurred.

Option 2

The middle executes a drag-down with the link and splits out; the link (as acting half) passes to the splitting middle (quickie), who looks to beat the retreating defender on the outside.

Option 3

The middle executes a drag-down with the link and splits out; the link (as acting half) passes away from the splitting middle to the middle on the other side of the field to where the ruck occurred. The middle receiving the ball runs a 'short'. They receive a short pass in the channel between the two middle defenders (with the intention of drawing both in to make the touch). The half follows their pass, wrapping or looping around the ball-carrier; if both defenders have been drawn in, the wrapping link will now be unmarked and a three-on-two will emerge on the opposite side of the field to where the ruck occurred.

Option 4

The middle executes a drag-down with the link and splits out; the link (as acting half) passes away from the splitting middle to the middle on the other side of the field to where the ruck occurred. The middle who is due to receive the ball positions themselves as if they are going to attack the channel between the two middle defenders (with the intention of keeping them from the far side of the field) and calls 'long'. Instead of a short pass between the two middle defenders, the half makes a long, flat pass to the outside channel. As the half passes the ball, the middle receiving the pass makes a sharp change of direction to run onto the ball. With the initial positioning, the flat pass and the sharp change of direction, the middle receiving the ball is hoping to keep the defenders on the side of the field where the ruck occurred and exploit the space on the other side of the field.

Further options

The middle who calls the short receives the ball and dummies a pass to the wrapping player before attacking the defender who made the initial touch; following a short (where the ball is passed to the wrapping middle) or a long, the ball-carrier attacks the outside of their defender before cutting with their link.

PLAYS ROOTED IN 33s WITH THE MIDDLE SPLITTING WITH THEIR MOMENTUM

The pattern underpinning the following options involves a middle (3) executing a drag-down with the other middle (3), splitting out once they have initiated the touch and rucked the ball (moving with their momentum).

Option 1

The middle executes a drag-down with the other middle and splits out; the middle (as acting half) scoops, attacking the channel between the two defensive middles with the intention of breaking the defensive line without being touched or of running the line to effectively create a four-on-three on the side of the field to which the splitting middle is moving.

Option 2

The middle executes a drag-down with the other middle and splits out; the middle (as acting half) passes to the splitting middle (quickie), who looks to beat the retreating defender on the outside.

Option 3

The middle executes a drag-down with the middle and splits out; the middle (as acting half) passes away from the splitting middle to the link on the other side of the field to where the ruck occurred. The link receiving the ball runs a 'short'. They receive a short pass in the channel between the defensive middle and link (with the intention of drawing both in to make the touch). The half follows their pass, wrapping or looping around the ball-carrier; if both defenders have been drawn in, the wrapping middle will now be unmarked and a two-on-one will emerge on the opposite side of the field to where the ruck occurred.

Option 4

The middle executes a drag-down with the middle and splits out; the middle (as acting half) passes away from the splitting middle to the link on the other side of the field to where the ruck occurred. The link who is due to receive the ball positions themselves as if they are going to attack the channel between the defensive link and middle (with the intention of keeping them from the far side of the field) and calls 'long'. Instead of a short pass between the defensive link and middle, the half makes a long, flat pass to the outside channel. As the half passes the ball, the link receiving the pass makes a sharp change of direction to run on to the ball. With the initial positioning, the flat pass and the sharp change of direction, the link receiving the ball is hoping to keep the defenders on the side of the field where the ruck occurred and exploit the space on the other side of the field, beating the defensive link on their outside to either score or execute a two-on-one.

Further options

The link who calls the short receives the ball and dummies a pass to the wrapping player before attacking the inside shoulder of their defender.

PLAYS ROOTED IN 33 WITH THE MIDDLE SPLITTING AGAINST THEIR MOMENTUM

The pattern underpinning the following options involves a middle (3) initiating the touch and rucking the ball on the defender marking them and then splitting back to the same side of the field on which they were originally standing (which is why this movement is called a 'samo'). This is a more difficult pattern to perfect as it involves the players initiating the touch moving against their natural momentum having rucked the ball.

Option 1

The middle initiates the touch on their defender and executes a samo (splitting back to the side in which they originally stood); the middle (as acting half) scoops, attacking the channel between the two defensive middles with the intention of breaking the defensive line without being touched or of running the line to effectively create a four-on-three on the side of the field to which the splitting middle is moving.

Option 2

The middle executes a samo and splits back to the side of the field in which they originally stood; the middle (as acting half) passes to the splitting middle who looks to beat the retreating defender on whom they initiated the touch on their outside.

Option 3

The middle executes a samo and splits back to the side of the field in which they originally stood; the middle (as acting half) passes away from the splitting middle to the link on the other side of the field to where the ruck occurred. The link receiving the ball runs a 'short'. They receive a short pass in the channel between the defensive middle and link (with the intention of drawing both in to make the touch). The half follows their pass, wrapping or looping around the ball-carrier; if both defenders have been drawn in, the wrapping middle will now be unmarked and a two-on-one will emerge on the opposite side of the field to where the ruck occurred.

Option 4

The middle executes a samo and splits back to the side of the field in which they originally stood; the middle (as acting half) passes away from the splitting middle to the link on the other side of the field to where the ruck occurred. The link who is due to receive the ball positions themselves as if they are going to attack the channel between the defensive link and middle (with the intention of keeping them from the far side of the field) and calls 'long'. Instead of a short pass between the defensive link and middle, the half makes a long, flat pass to the outside channel. As the half passes the ball, the link receiving the pass makes a sharp change of direction to run on to the ball. With the initial positioning, the flat pass and the sharp change of direction, the link receiving the ball is hoping to keep the defenders on the side of the field where the ruck occurred and exploit the space on the other side of the field, beating the defensive link on their outside to either score or execute a two-on-one.

7 PLAYING AT A HIGHER LEVEL – DEFENCE

At a high level of touch, coaches and players will have an understanding of the effectiveness and limits of defensive systems and which best suit the ability and skill level of their team. They will also be able to assess an opposition and see how they prefer to attack. Ultimately coaches and players need to develop the ability to estimate the vulnerability of their defence when it comes up against an opposition's attacking strategy. The major challenge comes when a coach or team realise that they are very vulnerable and look to adjust their defence accordingly. The following are methods of defending that teams use to a lesser or greater extent depending on the opposition they are playing and the strengths and weaknesses of that attacking side. As with the other defensive systems discussed in this book they are not perfect; but even if they make scoring just a little bit more difficult they could determine the outcome of a match.

Strong link defence

Attacking sides will often try to manipulate the defensive middles to pull them out of position – or to effectively do so through fatigue by consistently targeting them and getting them to complete a heavy defensive workload. To keep the middles fresh and help them retain their defensive shape, defences often operate a 'strong link' defensive system. Strong link defence involves the links on the outside of both middles standing tight to them. The links attempt to make as many of the middles' touches as they can by establishing (and communicating) the point beyond which the middle need not chase as the link is being 'strong' and giving them support. For example, if a ball-carrier attacks the middle on their outside shoulder – but does so at too obtuse an angle – they run into the link (who holds their tight position) and makes the touch. Thus the middle avoids unnecessary work.

Figure 7.1 In this example the left-hand attacking middle has attacked the player defending them at too obtuse an angle. The defensive link holds a tight position to the defensive middle and makes the touch on the ball-carrier.

It is important to note that the link retains defensive responsibility for their short side. If the attacker outside the ball-carrier receives the ball, the link must protect the channel now being attacked. For the link to be 'strong' effectively, they must not start in a position that is too wide. If they do so they will have to start to move to offer their support to the middle and, having generated infield momentum, it will be almost impossible for them to become an effective defender of the channel on their outside if required. Close initial positioning to the middle enables the link to help their middle avoid over-chasing and becoming vulnerable to a step or cut; and it also leaves them able to protect their short side.

DRILL 24

In an area 50 metres wide (the full width of a pitch) and approximately 20 metres deep (from the score-line out) six defenders play against six attackers. The width of the playing area is divided into three sections; initially the middle section should be approximately 25 metres wide and the two sections on the outside should be approximately 12.5 metres wide. Only the defensive middles are allowed inside the middle section – the defensive links and wings stand in the two outer sectors. The attackers have complete freedom of movement and attack the defenders' score-line. The links are instructed to help the middle defenders by making touches on their behalf where possible and therefore stand as close to the inner sector as they are allowed.

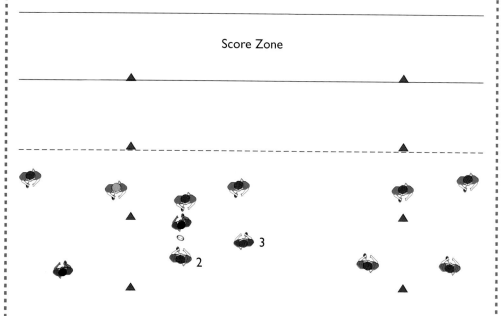

Figure 7.2 In this example the defensive links are very wide leaving the middles exposed. The link (2) is about to pick up the ball from acting half. They could run a short with the middle (3); scoop between the two defensive middles; or put the ball through the hands to the far attacking link. Any of these options is likely to result in a score.

Very quickly it will become apparent that the two defensive middles are hugely vulnerable – they have a large area to defend between the two of them and the attackers should exploit this to their advantage. The middles should feel very exposed and the links should be frustrated that they cannot be more helpful. Having rotated the defenders so that all players have the opportunity to briefly defend in both the middle and link positions, the middle sector is reduced to between 16 and 17 metres in width (and the two outside sectors accordingly decreased in size). The same rules apply – only the defensive middles are allowed in the middle section and the links are instructed to help the middle defenders by making touches on their behalf if the attackers enter their zone and to therefore stand as close to the inner sector as they are allowed. Defending in these conditions should be substantially easier for the middles; the links will make more touches on their behalf (without chasing infield) and the middles have less area to cover in defence.

This drill conditions links to avoid chasing infield to give the middles assistance at the same time as establishing how useful they can be if they take up a close, 'strong' position to the middles and take responsibility for making the touch on attackers where possible. The drill can be modified by changing the size of the sectors, and the danger of trying to play strong link defence with the middles defending too small an area can be illustrated by significantly reducing the size of the middle sector. In this scenario, the links (and wings) become very vulnerable on their outside which can be exploited by the attackers simply passing the ball down the line or running a D-cut.

High middle-link defence

High middle-link defence is not to be confused with strong link defence. High middle-link defence involves one middle assuming a more advanced position when the defence is within ten metres of the score-line they are defending. The advanced middle takes responsibility for making the touch on either attacking middle within the middle sector of the pitch. They will protect their short side by pulling their corner so they must be disciplined and not allow themselves to be pulled too far infield. The other defensive middle assumes a deeper set position close to the point the defence will have to retreat to once a touch has been made; they are very aware that they may be needed to instantly shut the channel between themselves and the advanced middle. This position is known as being 'in the pocket' of the advanced middle. The side of the field where the middle is in the pocket is open to attack because of the space conceded to the attacking side; therefore the link on that side of the field advances with the middle furthest from them in order to close down the space and pressurise the attacking team.

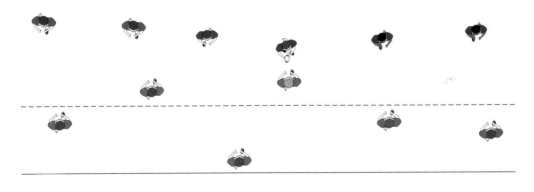

Score Zone

Figure 7.3 In this example the right defensive middle and left defensive link advance while the left defensive middle hangs back in the pocket. The right middle looks to make midfield touches, the left middle is ready to close the channel between the middles if the attackers look to accelerate into it while the right middle is retreating to the right-hand corner (the short side).

High middle-link defence is designed to close down the attack's options. If an attacking team shows a preference for attacking the defence's right-hand side (which many teams do, as the majority of players are right-handed and have a better long pass in that direction), the right defensive middle and left defensive link would advance; the right defensive middle would look to make the touch on either attacking middle near the centre of the field. This means that the defence will always be pulling to their right-hand corner and chasing out to where the attack prefers to pass, reducing this attacking play as an effective option. Alternatively, if an attacking team shows a preference for attacking the defence's left-hand side, the left defensive middle would look to make the touch on either attacking middle near the centre of the field. This means that the defence will always be pulling to their left-hand corner and chasing out to where the attack prefers to pass, reducing this attacking play as an effective option.

If a nominated middle is looking to make the touch and thus always pull to a particular corner, the attack will try to use this to their advantage. For example, the defence has nominated their right-hand middle to advance and make midfield touches as they know the attack favours a 33 (middle dropping for middle) with the middle who rucked the ball splitting towards the defence's right to receive the ball from the acting half. The attack observes in the early stages of a game that the defence's actions are nullifying an attacking play. In the second half of the game, the attack still runs a 33 and the rucking middle continues to split towards the defence's right-hand side. However, as the splitting middle receives the pass from the acting half they step back – against their momentum and that of the defence – to attack the right-hand defensive middle's inside shoulder (which is a channel opening up due to the right-hand middle's outward movement).

To protect this potential vulnerability, the left-hand defensive middle must be in a position to shut immediately. Hence they do not advance quickly upfield to keep pace with the right-hand middle. Instead they advance as slowly as allowed by the referee in order to be back onside as soon as possible once the touch has been made, ready to shut the channel (which is already their responsibility if the other middle makes the touch) as quickly as they can if required.

The advanced middle should avoid being pulled infield to make the touch – the intention of this system is, after all, for the advanced middle to protect their short side (the outside). However, if this does occur and the attack looks to exploit the outside, the middle in the pocket can undercut the advanced middle and chase to the outside while the advanced middle retreats into the channel vacated by their teammate. Similarly, if the advanced link is beaten on their outside, the middle in the pocket can undercut the advanced link and chase to the outside while the advanced link retreats into the middle channel.

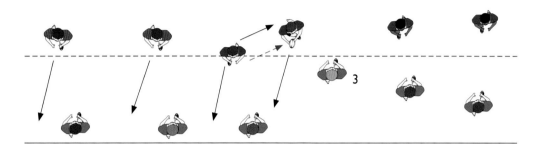

Score Zone

Figure 7.4 The defensive middle (3) made the touch and is retreating five metres towards their right to protect the short side. The middle who initiated the touch split to the defence's right and received the ball from the acting half; they have stepped against their momentum, between the two middles. The left-hand defensive middle in the pocket must be ready to advance and shut down this movement instantly to avoid conceding.

DRILL 25

Two teams of six face each other in a condensed space (approximately 15 metres deep and 30 metres across). Players on both sides are not allowed to run, only walk. At first, possession of the ball is limited to the two attacking middles, who may pass the ball to each other and move around as if attacking. The nominated middle and link advance – in this example, the defence's right-hand middle and left-hand link. The right-hand middle makes the touch if they can; however, one of the aims of this drill is to allow the nominated middle to gain a sense of when they should stop looking to make the touch, that is, if the left-hand attacking middle has the ball and moves a long way to the left-hand side of the field (as the defence looks upfield). It is not the intention for the nominated middle to be pulled infield before having to pull a corner to the right-hand side. The advanced defensive middle must establish with his advanced link the point at which the link must make the touch on the advanced middle's behalf. The two defensive middles must also establish when and where the advanced middle will make the touch and retreat straight back in a line as the defensive middle in the pocket undercuts them and chases out to the advanced middle's short side. This drill allows the defenders to gain an understanding and a visual image of their positioning. Defenders should rotate positions to become familiar with the defensive demands of all positions, particularly the middle and link. The drill can be developed so that the attack can pass the ball to any of the attacking six; the pace of the drill can be increased to pressurise decision-making, the area in which it is taking place is increased, etc.

8 REFINING HIGH LEVEL ATTACK

At the highest levels, players are likely to have a greater ability to observe the defence and attack weaknesses or openings as and when they emerge. With experience, application and good coaching, players will be able to select and execute the most effective action they can undertake in a situation as it develops; what Sir Clive Woodward described as T-CUP (thinking correctly under pressure). While specific moves can lead immediately to a scoring opportunity, they do not guarantee a score (as an individual defender can be exceptionally athletic or a good reader of the game and so cover the opening created by the attack). As a result, attackers need to understand the likely effect of their actions on a defence and the options that might emerge as one phase of play finishes and another starts. Coaches and players will attempt multi-phase plays where the intention of the first phase is to cause the defence to respond in their habitual fashion before exploiting the predicted position of the defenders in the second phase and beyond.

Driving: 3-2-1

This drive is designed to achieve many of the same outcomes as the previous patterns through greater use of the ball (rather than the running capability of the players). The numbers refer to the amount of passes executed in each phase; however, it is constructed on the premise of a side gaining possession with the ball on either the left or the right wing (as higher level teams will chose to finish their set of possession in a wide area of the field if they cannot manufacture a scoring opportunity). The '3' is merely indicative of the number of passes required to pass the ball from a roll ball on one wing (between the wing and link) and the link on the other side of the field and is not set in stone. If the roll ball that commences a set of possession is performed between the middle and the link, only two passes are required to achieve the same outcome, so players need to be aware that the purpose is to get the ball to the link on the far side of the field, not to complete three passes.

The ball is passed out to the link on the opposite side of the field to where the initial roll ball occurred; if this has been on the wing, it will take three passes to reach them. The link advances upfield and attempts to initiate the touch on the nearest defensive middle. The attacking middle who passed the ball to the rucking player becomes the acting half. The acting half passes the ball in the opposite direction to their previous pass, back to the attacking middle on the side of the field of the initial roll ball; they in turn pass the ball to the link on their outside who advances up the field and attempts to initiate the touch on the nearest middle defender. The '2' stage has been completed.

The attacking middle who passed the ball to the rucking link becomes the acting half. The acting half passes the ball in the opposite direction to their previous pass – to the other middle, who advances up the field and initiates the touch on their defender. The '1' stage has been completed.

If each stage has been executed effectively, the defensive middles will have been pulled in a variety of directions while the attacking middles (one of whom is rucking the ball and the other is the acting half at this last phase of play) are relatively fresh. Therefore the defence may be vulnerable to the acting half scooping; as it is the simplest option, it is preferable if it is feasible. Alternatively, the attack may decide to set up a specific attacking move having achieved good field position. The 3-2-1 drive has the advantage of spreading the play and causing the defence to chase one way and then the other without unnecessarily fatiguing the attackers as it is achieved through passing the ball rather than through the leg speed of the players. It also only uses three touches; if a scoop is not a feasible option then the attack still has three touches left with which to manufacture a scoring opportunity.

Attacking the score-line without momentum

When high-level teams find themselves close to the score-line they are attacking but without momentum (for example, against a defence that is set), they know it is not viable to attack the space behind the defence. The most space that can be attacked effectively is to the side of the defenders, so players aim to use the ruck as a platform to generate quick ball and lateral movement. In this they are helped by the rules that govern the actions of defenders near to their defensive line. Specifically, if one defender steps inside the five-metre zone in front of the score-line they are defending then every defender must keep advancing until the next touch is imminent; additionally a defender cannot change direction when retreating so as to influence play until they have retreated the full five metres and are deemed to be onside. The following patterns attempt to manipulate these rules when the attacking side has no momentum near the line they are attacking (for example, if they have just been given a penalty) in order to create space when a defence is well set.

LAZY CUT/SWITCH, DOWN, QUICKIE

The middle performs a lazy switch with the other middle, drawing the defenders out of the five-metre zone in front of the score-line. Having offloaded the ball, the passing middle decelerates to hold their field position in anticipation of becoming the acting half; having received the ball, the middle continues on their lateral line of movement infield for two or three strides, encouraging the defenders to step infield. The ball-carrier then steps sharply back out; they accelerate to attack the space between the defensive middle with the ambition of drawing both into the ruck. They initiate the touch on either defender and split out hard. The acting half picks the ball up and moves forward into the channel between the defensive middles – again, hoping to draw both players towards them – while looking to pass to the splitting player (quickie) as they attack the channel on the outside of their defender.

Figure 8.1 (a) The two middles have executed a lazy cut, and the ball-carrier has drifted infield;

(b) the ball-carrier steps back sharply towards the player who passed him the ball;

(c) the ball-carrier rucks the ball;

(d) and splits out hard with his momentum, receiving the ball from the acting half.

This same pattern can be performed by a middle and link. However, the middle-middle pattern has the advantage of the acting half and the splitting player attacking a greater area of the pitch and reducing the risk of running out of space. It also gives the splitting player more teammates on their outside to either put the ball through the hands or execute a drag-down with the link outside them.

LAZY CUT/SWITCH, DOWN, SAMO

The middle performs a lazy switch with the link on their outside, drawing the defenders out of the five-metre zone in front of the score-line. Having offloaded the ball, the middle continues along their lateral line of movement to get into the channel outside the defensive link; having received the ball the link continues on their lateral line of movement infield, encouraging the defenders to step infield and further away from the middle who offloaded the ball. The ball-carrier continues to drift in and executes a samo with the other middle (initiating the touch on their defender before splitting back to the side of the field on which they originally stood). The acting half passes to the splitting player as they attack the channel on the outside of the defender on whom they initiated the touch. If the defensive link steps in to help the middle close the channel, the ball-carrier passes to the player who offloaded the pass in the lazy switch and is now occupying a position outside the defensive link.

Figure 8.2 (a) The middle and the link perform a lazy cut;

(b) the ball-carrier drifts infield:

(c) the ball-carrier rucks the ball;

(d) the rucking player splits back to the side of the field on which they started;

(e) the acting half passes the ball to the splitting player;

(f) the ball-carrier attacks the space outside the defender who made the touch, with the original attacking middle on his outside.

LAZY CUT/SWITCH, DOWN, SAMO, STEP BACK

As a variation of the above, the middle performs a lazy switch with the link on their outside, drawing the defenders out of the five-metre zone in front of the score-line. Having offloaded the ball, the middle continues along their lateral line of movement to get into the channel outside the defensive link; having received the ball, the link continues on their lateral line of movement infield, encouraging the defenders to step infield and further away from the middle who offloaded the ball. The ball-carrier continues to drift in and executes a samo with the other middle (initiating the touch on their defender before splitting back to the side of the field on which they originally stood). The acting half passes to the splitting player as they attack the channel on the outside of the defender on whom they initiated the touch. Having made the defender react and also split out hard, the ball-carrier steps back, against their momentum, to attack the inside shoulder of the defender (the channel between the two defensive middles). If the defender cannot close the gap the attacker may score; or if the other defensive middle steps in to help their colleague, the ball-carrier can offload back to the acting half who will either be in a position to score themselves or have a three-on-two on the opposite side of the field to where the samo was executed.

Figure 8.3 (a) The link has just received the ball from a lazy cut and drifts infield;

(b) the ball-carrier's movement pulls the middle defenders together;

(c) the ball-carrier initiates the touch;

(d) before splitting back to the side of the field on which he originally stood;

(e) he receives the ball from the acting half and draws the defender to the outside;

(f) before stepping back infield, between the two middle defenders;

(g) drawing the two middle defenders leaves the acting half in space and an overlap.

The value of initiating the touch on the 'wrong' defender

The defensive patterns outlined have assumed that attackers will look to initiate the touch and execute rucks on the defender who is nominally marking them. Therefore initiating the touch on the 'wrong' defender can create confusion simply because it is unexpected; the attack benefits from doing that which the defence has not anticipated. For example, the attacking middles might look to execute a 33 – a drag-down with the rucking middle intending to split out once they have performed the roll ball. However, in the final seconds before initiating the touch, the ball-carrier drifts further towards the inside of the field and initiates the touch on the defensive middle furthest from them.

When the acting half picks up the ball they will almost certainly already be between the two defensive middles and if they look to attack the side of the field to which their fellow attacker is splitting they are likely to have a four-on-three overlap that has been achieved through minimal effort. If the splitting middle is immediately passed the ball by the acting half they will have more space than if they had initiated the touch on their own defender and so were splitting into the channel defended by the player who had been marking the acting half before the ruck was executed. If the defender on whom the touch was initiated chases hard to close this extra space, a channel may open up between the two defensive middles for the acting half to scoop through. Alternatively, if the splitting middle receives the ball and the space between the two defensive middles still does not close up, they will be vulnerable to a cut executed between the splitting middle and their outside link.

Similarly, the attacking middles may decide to execute a samo with the ball-carrier initiating the touch on the middle furthest away from them. They then step back towards the side of the field on which they originally stood. When the acting half picks up the ball they will be between the two defensive middles with the defender closest to them moving away. The acting half can pass to the splitting player. If the splitting player is highly agile they may have the opportunity to step back (against the direction they are splitting) and attack the channel between the two defensive middles and attempt to score or exploit the overlap their movements have created.

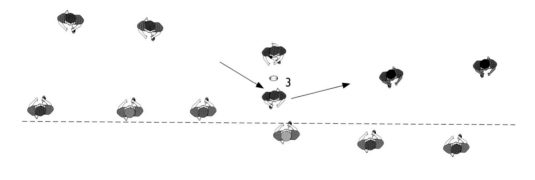

Score Zone

Figure 8.4 The middle (3) drifts on to the 'wrong' defender and rucks the ball, splitting towards the defence's right-hand side. When the acting half picks the ball up they have an instant overlap on the defence's right.

Figure 8.5 (a) The ball-carrier drifts on to the 'wrong' defender and rucks the ball;

(b) the rucking player splits back to the side of the field on which he originally stood and receives the pass from the acting half.

(c) the splitting player steps back against his momentum to attack between the two middle defenders; there is an overlap on the side of the field in which the acting half is standing.

Running a chop line

Lines of running are hugely important in all forms of rugby and the chop or screen pass is a concept used in both union and league. The intention is for potential receivers to move effectively off the ball to give the ball-carrier options while confusing defenders. For example, the middle and link execute a 32 (a drag-down). The acting half looks to pass the ball to the other side of the field to where the ruck occurred. Rather than a direct (and potentially predictable) pass to the middle, the link on the far side of the field 'chops', that is, they angle their run to attack the channel on the inside shoulder of the link defender nominally marking them. The attacking middle allows the link to run ahead of them before undercutting the run and accelerating into the channel on the outside shoulder of the defensive link. The link defender may hesitate or step in when they find they are simultaneously being attacked on both their inside and outside (they should always defend the outside channel). The acting half reads what the defence is doing before deciding who to pass to. If the defensive link stays out and the defensive middle hangs back, the ball is passed to the link angling inwards. If the defensive link hesitates or steps in, the ball is passed to the middle angling out. In the latter circumstance, the pass is made behind the back of the chopping link who screens the pass to the middle and continues to draw the defence out of position.

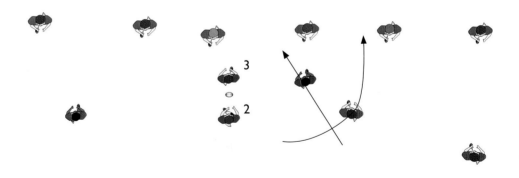

Figure 8.6 The chop line gives the acting half two possible passing options and isolates a defender, having a runner attacking the space outside each shoulder.

Doing the unexpected

Defences can become used to dealing with attacks 'going with the flow', that is, attacking outside channels in successive phases (32 quickie) or attacking the inside channels after having feinted to the outside first (33 samo, step back). A less common tactic – maybe all the more effective for being rare – is to attack the outside channels after having feinted to the inside first. In a one-on-one scenario the ball-carrier would look to beat a defender by stepping from in to out – in other words they would angle towards the infield before stepping to the outside, shifting the point of attack from the defender's inside shoulder to their outside shoulder. This would require the attacker to be in possession of an extremely effective side-step; or to have a significant pace advantage over the defender; or for the defender to make an error in chasing hard towards the infield and thereby handing an overlap to the attacking side without them having to work hard to achieve it. All of these scenarios are feasible but are difficult to plan. However, there are other ways in which attacking sides can play to feint towards the inside channels with the effect of making defenders move from out (protecting the short side) to in. The attacking side then has the opportunity to attack the space that has been created on the outside.

MOVEMENT INFIELD, HARD CUT OUTFIELD

The ball-carrying link steps infield to attack the space between the link defender and the nearest defensive middle; the intention is to draw the defensive link infield. The nearest attacking middle undercuts the run of the ball-carrying link and receives an offloaded pass from them. Having caught the ball, the cutting player accelerates into the channel between the defensive link and the defensive wing.

The intention of the pattern is to push the defence infield before cutting to the outside, with the receiver of the final pass accelerating into a channel that is being opened up for them by the defender's infield movement. The defence can also be moved infield prior to the middle cut by the attacking link cutting with the attacking wing who accelerates into the channel between the defensive link and defensive middle.

Figure 8.7 (a) The link attacks the space between the defensive link marking him and the nearest defensive middle.

(b) the attacking middle nearest to the ball-carrier undercuts the infield run of the ball-carrier and receives an offloaded pass from him; she accelerates into the channel between the defensive link and the defensive winger.

SAMO, STEP IN, CUT OUT

The middle executes a samo with the other middle and splits back to the side of the field in which they originally stood; the middle (as acting half) passes to the splitting middle. Having made the defender react and also split out hard, the ball-carrier steps back, against their momentum, to attack the inside shoulder of the defender (the channel between the two defensive middles). The acting half undercuts the run of the ball-carrier from whom they receive an offloaded pass; the acting half who is now carrying the ball accelerates into the channel between the defensive middle and defensive link ready to exploit the overlap that has been created on that side of the field.

Figure 8.8 (a) The ball-carrier initiates the touch on the defender marking him;

(b) he then splits back to the side of the field on which he started;

(c) and receives the ball from the acting half;

(d) the splitting player steps back, against his momentum, to attack the channel between the two defensive middles in order to draw the player marking him infield;

(e) the acting half undercuts the ball-carrier and receives an offloaded pass from him;

(f) the new ball-carrier accelerates into the space between the defensive middle and defensive link, exploiting the overlap he has created.

The intention of this pattern is again to push the defence infield before cutting to the outside, with the receiver of the final pass accelerating into a channel that is being opened up for them by the defender's infield movement. The acting half who cuts may have the opportunity to score, but if the defensive link and wing also move infield the channel may be closed down. However, they will still have an attacking link and wing on their outside and will have the opportunity to exploit a three-on-two overlap.

One method of doing the unexpected that some attackers adopt is initiating the touch by 'swiping' – batting at the hand or arm of the defender to put them off-balance and pushing them in the opposite direction from that in which the attacker intends to split. This creates more space for the attacker; but players should be aware that referees are empowered to penalise an attacker who initiates a touch in a way that puts the defender at a disadvantage. However, 'disadvantage' is a matter of interpretation and some referees will allow what others would penalise.

Figure 8.9 An attacking player 'swipes' at the defender making the touch and gains control over the timing of the ruck, upsetting the defender's balance.

9 FIT FOR TOUCH

There is a huge amount of information and advice available on developing fitness written by experts in their field. During my involvement with touch I have been fortunate to read and view the work of medical and fitness professionals whose insight into this field is greater than mine. The following briefly outlines some of the protocols I feel have most developed the fitness and athleticism of players. For more detail, I recommend investigating the work of experts in this field.

Aerobic base

Touch is a game that rarely stops and tournaments may require a number of games in a single day. Playing touch develops aerobic capacity but aerobic capacity needs to be developed in order to play at a high level. I strongly recommend interval training to develop VO_2 max for any aspiring touch player. Although a GPS heart-rate monitor, a running track or treadmill can be used to quantify precisely how far an athlete runs or how hard they are working, a simple rule of thumb would be to run for between three and five minutes at a pace that can only be sustained for the duration of the interval. If the pace can be maintained for longer than five minutes it is unlikely that the athlete is working hard enough; if the interval is for less than three minutes it is not going to effectively develop the VO_2 max of the athlete. After the interval, the athlete rests for the same length of time as the interval (a work-to-rest ratio of 1:1). Three to five sets of intervals executed once a week will see significant development of the aerobic base required for touch.

Plyometrics

While aerobic capacity helps players to repeat their level of physical effort in the course of a game or a day of tournament touch, speed, agility and quickness are attributes capable of changing the course of a match. The more scores a team can achieve through simple patterns of play (for example, beating a defender on their outside, scooping from acting half and passing to an unmarked player or stepping inside a defender and diving), the more likely they are to win. Bodyweight exercises in isolation and as part of plyometric circuits are the most straightforward way to develop speed and power. They require minimal equipment, can be executed in any space and closely resemble the physical movements required in a game. Effective exercises include;

- Press-ups with the focus on a slow lowering to the floor and an explosive drive phase, straightening the arms.

- Bicycles: lying on their back with their hands on the side of their heads, the athlete raises their legs approximately six inches off the floor. The athlete uses their core muscles to drive their right elbow forward and their left knee towards their head; they meet over the athlete's midsection. The athlete returns to the starting position slowly before executing the same dynamic movement with the left elbow and right knee.

- Crossovers: in a press-up position the athlete drives the left leg forward and across the body so that the left knee comes close to or touches the right elbow before returning to the starting position. At this point the athlete drives the right leg forward and across the body until the right knee comes close to or touches the left elbow. The focus is on the drive phase forward.

- Step-downs: using a surface approximately knee-high. Standing on the box on one leg, the athlete lowers the other leg until the toes touch the floor; the weight of the athlete is constantly through the leg on the box. Once the toes touch the floor, the athlete explosively straightens the leg on the box.

- Box jumps: the athlete stands in front of a box – the higher the box, the more challenging the exercise. The athlete jumps vertically and forward, attempting to land softly on the top of the box. The athlete jumps to the floor, again attempting to land softly on the ground.

Exercises can be undertaken in numerous combinations of repetitions, sets and rest periods.

Speed, agility and quickness (SAQ)

While plyometrics help to develop speed, sprinting and sprint intervals are also important. These can be undertaken in numerous combinations of repetitions and rest periods, for example, 10-, 20- or 40-metre sprints with 30 seconds' rest, repeated ten times. Speed endurance is an important building block for speed and so 400-metre to 600-metre intervals on a 1:1 work-to-rest ratio can be very effective. Agility is also advantageous. In my experience, athletes who are undertaking the kind of training outlined above find that their agility improves as they become quicker and develop stronger core muscles. Drills that involve sudden and unexpected changes of direction over five to ten metres, constantly changing direction, also help.

In addition to the above, the more touch an individual plays, the more their body adapts to the demands of the sport. Playing develops agility as attackers and defenders try to score or prevent scores. On top of any training programme I would strongly recommend any athlete to play as much as they can to develop their physical capacity for the sport while simultaneously developing their level of skill.

INDEX